NYSTCE®

Physical Education Practice Questions

Mometrix
TEST PREPARATION

DEAR FUTURE EXAM SUCCESS STORY

First of all, **THANK YOU** for purchasing Mometrix study materials!

Second, congratulations! You are one of the few determined test-takers who are committed to doing whatever it takes to excel on your exam. **You have come to the right place.** We developed these practice tests with one goal in mind: to deliver you the best possible approximation of the questions you will see on test day.

Standardized testing is one of the biggest obstacles on your road to success, which only increases the importance of doing well in the high-pressure, high-stakes environment of test day. Your results on this test could have a significant impact on your future, and these practice tests will give you the repetitions you need to build your familiarity and confidence with the test content and format to help you achieve your full potential on test day.

Your success is our success

We would love to hear from you! If you would like to share the story of your exam success or if you have any questions or comments in regard to our products, please contact us at **800-673-8175** or **support@mometrix.com**.

Thanks again for your business and we wish you continued success!

Sincerely,
The Mometrix Test Preparation Team

TABLE OF CONTENTS

Practice Test #1

Selected Response

1. Multiple researchers have found that student attitudes toward physical activity are helped by mastery-oriented learning climates, which include teachers' using effective learning strategies, but are hindered by performance-oriented climates. Of the following, which is part of a performance-oriented climate rather than a mastery-oriented one?

a. Student preferences for challenging tasks
b. Student positive attitudes about the class
c. Student ability and norms instead of work
d. Student effort is believed to bring success

2. Professional development at its best accomplishes which of these?

a. It primarily improves the teacher's own knowledge and skills.
b. It improves both a teacher's and his or her colleagues' expertise.
c. It primarily improves the expertise of the teacher's colleagues.
d. It improves teaching practices primarily at the classroom level.

3. A man with a history of bipolar I disorder and opiate abuse reports suicidal thoughts with a plan to his therapist. He was recently in a car accident and broke his leg. The patient says that he had one suicide attempt by overdose five years ago. He is actively using intravenous drugs and has a history of sexual trauma during childhood. Which factor listed is NOT a risk factor of suicide?

a. History of childhood sexual abuse
b. Active substance abuse
c. Past suicide attempt
d. His recent car accident

4. Out of 30 students, 10 are advanced, 10 are intermediate, and 10 are beginners. Which of the following strategies best accommodates mixed-ability students for skill development and refinement?

a. Skill choice
b. Varied skill circuits
c. Combined skill grouping
d. Partner advanced and beginner students

5. Kenya is having difficulty with balance and coordination skills in the gymnastic routines. Which perceptual motor ability may be underdeveloped?

a. Hearing
b. Vision
c. Touch sensitivity
d. Audiation

6. Among the most prevalent challenges to kindergarten through Grade 12 physical education, which has recently become even more challenging than the others?

a. Inadequate resources and parental support
b. Overly large class sizes and teacher burnout
c. Violence, student drug abuse, and discipline
d. Reductions in school curriculum times for physical education

7. Which of the following best describes the purpose of teaching chasing, fleeing, and dodging games?

a. To prepare students for invasion games
b. To develop effort and spatial awareness
c. To teach locomotor movements
d. To teach non-locomotor movements

8. Which of the following is classified as a non-locomotor skill?

a. Running
b. Jumping
c. Climbing
d. Dodging

9. Among progressive-resistance exercises, which of the following uses the largest number and variety of equipment?

a. Free weight work
b. Partner resistance
c. Body weight training
d. Circuit weight training

10. Kimberly is not demonstrating opposition during the overhand throw. Which of the following techniques will promote the desired outcome?

a. Telling her she needs to step with the opposite foot
b. Telling her to practice daily
c. Telling her to work with a partner
d. The teacher should recognize that all students will not master every skill and move on

11. Excess body fat increases the risk of poor health. Which of the following activities aids in establishing a healthy body composition?

a. Increase physical activity when eating foods with fat
b. Avoid foods with fat
c. Cross-train and monitor food intake
d. Read food labels and move more

12. Which of the following indicates an effective muscular endurance training program?

a. Increasing the rep count over time
b. Increasing soreness over time
c. Maintaining the rep count over time
d. Increasing the weight over time

13. Individuals with low health literacy are often less likely to comply with a physician's medical directions, which could result in adverse health outcomes. Which strategy should a physician use to confirm a patient's comprehension?

a. The physician should summarize critical information at the end of the appointment.
b. The physician should use diagrams or draw pictures to explain complex medical concepts.
c. The physician should offer the patient multiple types of educational materials (e.g., pamphlet, visual diagram, video).
d. The physician should ask the patient to teach-back the health instructions.

14. What is the first step in the DECIDE model?

a. Define the criteria
b. Decide to act
c. Develop a plan of action
d. Define the problem

Refer to the following for question 15:

Research shows that exercise lowers the risk of high blood pressure, stroke, and heart disease. In particular, aerobic exercise has been proven to protect the cardiovascular system.

15. What is true about other health benefits of exercise?

a. Exercise lowers the risk of all kinds of cancers.
b. Exercise cannot change the risk of dementia.
c. Exercise lowers the risk for Type 1 diabetes.
d. Exercise lowers the risk of breaking bones.

16. Which of the following movement concepts help facilitate relationships with objects in the environment?

a. forward and backward
b. over and under
c. straight and curved
d. strong and light

17. Why is it important for individuals to know the health history of their parents prior to engaging in physical activity?

a. Predisposed health conditions
b. Previous musculoskeletal injuries
c. Effects of physical activity response
d. Physical activity readiness questionnaire

18. Which of the following agencies would be most helpful to someone who wants to know more about nutrition?

a. FDA
b. USDA
c. EPA
d. DOT

19. Which of the following steps used in jazz dance is similar to the gallop?

a. chasse
b. axel
c. ball change
d. the drop

20. Which of the following explains the importance of discipline when engaging in recreational activities?

a. The rules of engagement are unclear.
b. There is no one to monitor activity.
c. The outcome goals are unclear.
d. Goals vary for each individual.

21. Which of the following fitness activities are students engaged in when participating in orienteering?

a. Walking, hiking, and swimming
b. Walking, cycling, and swimming
c. Walking, jogging, and running
d. Swimming, cycling, and running

22. Which objective strategy helps students evaluate their cardiorespiratory fitness?

a. The talk test
b. Track resting heart rate
c. Work at the target heart rate
d. Reflection

23. Among elements of the FITT principle, which one is determined by two of the others?

a. How long each workout session should last
b. How to ensure overload without overwork
c. How often to work out for stress plus rest
d. How training is cardio, resistance, or both

24. An assertive person is LEAST likely to do which of the following?

a. Use "I" statements to express his or her feelings
b. Seek to understand a speaker's point of view
c. Withhold his or her opinions or feelings from others
d. Set boundaries with others

25. Body mass index (BMI) calculates an individual's proportion of body fat to height and weight. Which of the following BMI ranges corresponds to a normal body composition?

a. 18.5 or less
b. 25.0 to 29.9
c. 18.5 to 24.9
d. 30 or more

26. Among social, emotional, environmental, and health factors that affect motor development and performance, which of the following is the *best* example of the impact of social factors?

a. A student's insecurities impede participation in physical activities.
b. Many students would rather play video games than physical ones.
c. Poor home living conditions limit a student's physical activity and fitness.
d. A student's illness or disability makes physical activity challenging.

27. Positive health behaviors include regularly being physically active, getting a good night's sleep, and eating a nutritious diet. However, adolescent health especially realizes the impact of factors influencing these. Which choice accurately represents one such factor?

a. On a typical day, teens get almost 30 percent of their calories from sugars and solid fats.
b. On a typical day, almost 25 percent of teens watch TV recreationally for three hours or more.
c. On a typical day, parental support and sibling activities have no influence on teens.
d. On a typical day, most high school students sleep fewer hours nightly than needed.

28. Which of the following activities improve flexibility and posture?

a. isometric training
b. plank exercises
c. free weight training
d. running

29. The teacher probed students on how and when they get open during a game of soccer. Which of the following is the aim of the teacher's question?

a. to teach affective skills
b. to teach psychomotor skills
c. to teach tactical skills
d. to teach transfer skills

30. Which of these is true about characteristics of developmentally appropriate physical education?

a. Children are more different individually than they are alike.
b. Children go through all of the same stages of development.
c. Children go through developmental stages in varying order.
d. Children develop at identical or similar rates.

31. Which of the following strategies helps accommodate multiple abilities in physical education classes?

a. Teaching to the outcome
b. Providing extensions
c. Employing standards-based instruction
d. Incorporating differentiation

32. Which of the following is a short-term effect of exercise on the cardiorespiratory system?

a. Lower resting heartrate
b. Increased vital capacity
c. Increased tidal volume
d. Greater stroke volume

33. In addition to physical activity, which of the following activities has been shown to help manage stress?

a. Drinking red wine
b. Getting adequate sleep
c. Watching television
d. Drinking caffeine

34. Prenatal, infant, and child motor development progresses from the head down. This is known as:

a. Cephalocaudal development
b. Proximodistal development
c. Mediolateral development
d. Intellectual development

35. A student practices in isolation how to hit a field hockey ball. Once the student's skills improve, the PE teacher places the student in a field hockey game. In terms of Knowledge of Performance (KP) and Knowledge of Results (KR), which is true about this example?

a. KP applies more to practice, KR more to a game.
b. KP applies more to a game, KR more to practice.
c. KP and KR apply equally to practicing and games.
d. Neither KP nor KR helps in practicing or a game.

36. Of the following beliefs common among high school students about exercise, nutrition, and health, which is accurate rather than a misconception or myth?

a. Eat simple carbs after exercising.
b. Everybody should take vitamins.
c. Drink eight glasses of water per day.
d. Vitamins supply greater energy.

Refer to the following for question 37:

A student playing as a goalie in soccer is having difficulty punting the ball. He takes two steps, drops the ball from waist height, leans back, and kicks the bottom of the ball with the toe of his shoe. During one of his attempts, he accidentally punts the ball at his teammate Tracy, causing her nose to begin bleeding.

37. Which of the following changes should the student make to improve his punt?

a. dropping the ball from head height
b. standing still while kicking
c. kicking with the shoelaces
d. leaning forward

38. Which of the following best describes the purpose of rhythmic activities?

a. To learn music tempo
b. To learn how to perform
c. To learn how to control the body
d. To learn the locomotor movements

39. Coach Wheelock refuses to let the girls on the school's basketball team play with the boys in physical education because he says the boys play too rough. Which of the following practices does Coach Wheelock exhibit?

a. Safety for injury prevention
b. Gender discrimination
c. Favoritism towards the boys
d. Gender stereotypes

40. The federal government defines basic elements of furthering student development through physical activity (PA) that PE programs and teachers promote. How are these elements structured to accomplish major PE goals?

a. Attaining participant developmental health outcomes enables creating optimum contexts for PA, which enables providing universal PA opportunities and access.
b. Creating optimum contexts for PA enables providing universal PA opportunities and access, which enables attaining participant developmental health outcomes.
c. Providing universal PA opportunities and access enables creating optimum contexts for PA, which enables attaining participant developmental health outcomes.
d. Attaining participant developmental health outcomes enables providing universal PA opportunities and access, which enables creating optimum contexts for PA.

41. Which of the following are the movement pathways used to teach locomotor movements?

a. straight, curved, zigzag
b. right, left, forward, diagonal
c. straight, forward, backward
d. zigzag, forward, backward

42. Ms. Jones collected students' dribbling skills tests data for five years and found many students were not proficient by the end of 8th grade. Which of the following is a logical next step for Ms. Jones to take to improve student dribbling outcomes?

a. Accepting that not all students will meet outcomes
b. Introducing dribbling skills sooner
c. Evaluating her instructional skill cues
d. Providing after-school instruction

43. According to Piaget's developmental theory, when do children show the first signs of symbolic function?

a. During the sensorimotor stage
b. During the preoperational stage
c. In the concrete operations stage
d. In the formal operations stage

44. A student is having difficulty staying afloat during the swimming unit. Which of the following identifies a potential problem and a solution to the student's issue?

a. The student has increased drag and needs to empty the air in their lungs
b. The student has high buoyancy and needs to empty the air in their lungs
c. The student lacks drag and needs to fill up their lungs with air
d. The student lacks buoyancy and needs to fill up their lungs with air

45. A student who is practicing a new skill that is outside of her comfort zone but is excited about the prospect of accomplishing this feat may be experiencing which type of stress?

a. Eustress
b. Acute stress
c. Distress
d. Academic stress

46. Regarding physical, emotional, and social factors that influence personal physical health, which of the following is true?

a. Anxiety and depression cause sleep and diet problems but not cardiovascular troubles.
b. Stress and family dysfunction cause emotional problems, not physical illness.
c. Air pollution can aggravate asthma but is not actually found to cause asthma.
d. People can overeat and be overweight, and yet still suffer from malnutrition.

47. The teacher observes students daily and compares movement to the skill cues or model to provide student feedback. Which assessment strategy is the teacher using?

a. Formative assessment
b. Summative assessment
c. Assessment for learning
d. Assessment as learning

48. Which of these is NOT a typical effect of substance abuse on student behavior?

a. A shy student becomes more sociable and popular.
b. An outgoing student becomes withdrawn.
c. An inhibited student becomes more impulsive.
d. A student finds long-term, sustained academic success.

49. Which of the following agencies sets the national K-12 physical education standards?

a. CAEP
b. GOPHER
c. NASPE
d. SHAPE

50. According to group dynamics theory, ________ groups are formed voluntarily among individuals with similar interests and shared goals.

a. friendship
b. interest
c. task
d. functional

51. Which of the following is considered a best practice for continuous aerobic training bouts for elementary-aged students?

a. 60-minute bouts
b. 45-minute bouts
c. 30-minute bouts
d. 15-minute bouts

52. When designing, choosing, modifying, and sequencing game activities, what should PE teachers have as their main purpose(s)?

a. To ensure that students remain occupied
b. To enhance skills practice and enjoyment
c. To ensure student behavior management
d. To enhance student enjoyment primarily

53. Of the following motor skills, which do babies or toddlers typically develop the latest?

a. Play "pattycake"
b. Pull up to stand
c. Jumping in place
d. The pincer grasp

54. Which of the following combined motor skills is on the upper end of the skill progression continuum?

a. Skipping baseline to baseline
b. Running 400 meters
c. Dribbling a soccer ball
d. Jumping over an obstacle

55. Typical safety guidelines for ascending climbing ropes in portable or permanent installations on school or commercial sites are best reflected by which choice?

a. A working phone is only needed for installations outside of the school.
b. An accessible first aid kit is unnecessary at installations within schools.
c. All climbing ropes are compatible with all activities, plus belay devices.
d. Equipment must meet standards and be made for the planned activity.

56. The President's Council on Physical Fitness and Sports (2009) identifies five levels of responsibility as positive youth development goals, including the choices below. Of these, which is most related to the self-management skill of self-direction?

a. Respecting the feelings and rights of others
b. Trying out new tasks and persisting at tasks
c. Independent work, progressive goal setting
d. Democratic approaches to resolving conflict

57. Which of the following physiological adaptations do cardiovascular activities induce?

a. less reliance on glucose
b. heart size increases
c. decrease in blood volume
d. lactic acid build-up

58. Among tactics typically employed by domestic abusers to control their victims, what is destroying the victim's property an example of?

a. Isolation
b. Humiliation
c. Denying
d. Intimidation

59. A student recently joined a fitness center and wants to hire a personal trainer. Which of the following should the student use to evaluate the quality of the personal trainer?

a. referrals
b. body builder experience
c. a college degree
d. certification

60. Which of the following is a logical next step after students have learned the rules and basic skills for lacrosse?

a. Game observation
b. Game analysis
c. Offensive skills
d. Small-sided games

61. A century of research into motor development has yielded four major principles. Which choice most accurately reflects one of these principles?

a. Children are like adults, only smaller.
b. Children differ completely by gender.
c. Good things are earned.
d. Children have perfect bodies, or not.

62. A high school student learns the principle of available force, and by applying it, recognizes similarities among different sports. Which statement correctly reflects a related observation?

a. In the broad jump, the takeoff can be too fast for the best force.
b. In golf, the best results can be achieved by swinging the fastest.
c. In this principle, variations in force and movement speed match.
d. In the shot put, movement in the final thrust has no speed limit.

63. A spectator passes out during the football game and the CPR certified PE teacher is called to help. Which of the following steps should the PE teacher do first?

a. call 911
b. check the scene
c. check for breathing
d. start CPR

64. Which of the following is NOT a professional, legal, or ethical practice regarding sensitive issues?

a. Distributing parent permission forms before a sexual health education unit
b. Sharing information with a caregiver about a student's question related to contraception
c. Reporting sexual abuse
d. Offering professional development training about child protection issues

65. "Sliding vs. deciding" is a concept used to describe the practice or absence of intentional decision-making in relationships, usually with specific regard to romantic relationships. A sliding decision may be the result of impulsivity, internal and/or external pressure to comply (e.g., personal or cultural values, peer pressure), poor communication, or convenience. Each of the following is a strategy to prevent sliding in a romantic relationship EXCEPT:

a. Discussing personal values and relationship goals early in the relationship
b. Exploring the advantages and disadvantages of a mutual decision before it is made
c. Dividing decision-making responsibilities equitably between partners
d. Establishing clear and healthy relationship boundaries with your romantic partner

66. Students in class have a cross country meet tomorrow. Which of the following recommendations will help students prepare?

a. "Take a practice run on the course."
b. "Take a practice run at a lower intensity."
c. "Get more rest and increase fat intake."
d. "Get more rest and increase carbohydrate intake."

67. Which of these is most accurate when comparing inline roller skates and quad roller skates?

a. Inline and quad skates only differ in wheel positioning.
b. Inline skates are more maneuverable than quad skates.
c. Inline skates are faster and help skaters avoid small obstacles.
d. Inline skates are only for outdoor, quads for indoor use.

68. Among the components of health-related physical fitness, _____ is the bridge between _____ and _____.

a. Muscular endurance; muscular strength; cardiovascular endurance
b. Cardiovascular endurance; muscular strength; muscular endurance
c. Muscular strength; cardiovascular endurance; muscular endurance
d. Cardiovascular endurance; body composition; flexibility or mobility

69. Valerie is using the decision-making process to pick a new primary care doctor. She has compiled a list of potential doctors, made sure they were covered by her insurance, and read reviews about each doctor online. Which of these should be her next step?

a. Identify alternatives
b. Take action
c. Choose among alternatives
d. Identify the decision

70. Which of the following strategies is recommended when selecting weight training activities for beginning students?

a. Utilizing dumbbells
b. Utilizing bodyweight
c. Utilizing a one-repetition max strength test
d. Alternating light and heavy weight

71. Among the benefits to students of teamwork in sports, which of these is LEAST applicable?

a. Communication and cooperation
b. Socializing in less sedentary ways
c. Learning to win above everything
d. Valuing commitment, dedication

72. According to attachment theory, a person whose parents rejected his or her social-emotional needs during childhood is most likely to develop which of the following attachment styles that is characterized by independence, intolerance of close relationships, and evasion of emotional situations?

a. Secure attachment
b. Anxious attachment
c. Disorganized attachment
d. Avoidant attachment

73. A middle school has recently seen a major uptick in the frequency of fights between students throughout the past month. Which of the following is the best policy response to implement in this situation to prevent further violent incidents?

a. Increasing the security presence on campus
b. Implementing a zero-tolerance policy that assigns suspensions to anyone involved in fights
c. Implementing a universal school-based prevention program for violent or aggressive behavior
d. Performing regular behavioral risk assessments to identify and discipline students at risk for violence

74. Which of the following is an example of how emotional/behavioral factors can affect young children's levels of physical activity and fitness?

a. A child diagnosed with ADHD is physically so overactive that he becomes exhausted.
b. A child diagnosed with asthma needs monitoring for breathing problems in exercise.
c. A child diagnosed with diabetes needs exercise watched and coordinated with diet.
d. A child diagnosed with disabilities needs adaptive equipment for physical activities.

75. Which of the following high school trends have impacted the shift away from team sports to health-related fitness in physical education programs?

a. technology
b. childhood obesity
c. adult preparation
d. health promotion

76. In which of the following school levels is movement education most appropriate?

a. Pre-kindergarten
b. Elementary school
c. Middle school
d. High school

77. Of the following choices, which one most describes a stage of motor learning associated with the age period of adolescence?

a. Purposeful movements develop beyond simple reflexes.
b. Motor patterns of increasing complexity are developing.
c. Motor patterns gain increasing automaticity and fluidity.
d. Ability, motivation, and practice influence development.

78. After graduating from high school, Omar decides to pursue a degree in music theory. His parents share that they are disappointed with his career choice and attempt to persuade him to change his mind; however, they eventually tell Omar that they can "live with it." All three acknowledge their differences in opinion and do not discuss his decision further. This scenario is an example of which characteristic of healthy relationships?

a. Acceptance
b. Understanding
c. Tolerance
d. Empathy

79. Using a lever gives a mechanical advantage (MA), expressed as the ratio of the power arm's length to the weight arm's length. In other words, MA = a ratio of motive force to resistive force. What is true about this principle?

a. If the quotient is <1, motive force is < resistive force.
b. If the quotient is >1, resistive force is > motive force.
c. If the quotient is =1, there is the greatest advantage.
d. If the quotient is >1, resistive force is < motive force.

80. A student sprains an ankle after landing from a balance beam jump. Which of the following is the first priority immediately after a student sprains an ankle?

a. Mobilizing the injury
b. Putting ice on the injury
c. Putting heat on the injury
d. Calling 911

81. Which of the following safety practices is recommended in dance?

a. dynamic warm-up
b. static movements
c. loose clothing
d. yoga stretches

82. Which component of health-related physical fitness is most dependent on the others?

a. Flexibility/mobility
b. Body composition
c. Cardiovascular endurance
d. Muscular strength

83. Which of the following best describes the appropriate duration training for a midfielder in soccer?

a. Long duration
b. Short duration
c. Intervals
d. Player specific

84. Tom is driving Louisa home after their first date. As they approach Louisa's house, Tom begins to make unwanted sexual advances toward Louisa. Which of the following is the LEAST effective strategy for refusing sexual advances?

a. Louisa remains quiet and hopes that Tom will pick up that she is uncomfortable.
b. Louisa tells Tom that she is not interested.
c. Louisa makes a joke to defuse the tension.
d. Louisa exits the car and heads to a neighbor's house until Tom leaves.

85. Which of these accurately reflects research findings on gender differences in early childhood motor development?

a. Preschool girls are found to be equally muscular as, but more physically mature than, boys are in preschool.
b. Preschool boys exhibit both more strength and coordination in large-muscle gross-motor skills than girls do.
c. Preschool girls exhibit more fine-motor skills, but less gross-motor coordination, than boys do in preschool.
d. Despite certain differences, preschool motor development between genders is more similar than different.

86. Which of the following biomechanical principles is illustrated during the roll portion in a forward roll?

a. angle of release
b. angular momentum
c. force
d. inertia

87. Which of the following best describes the differences between motor learning and motor performance?

a. Motor performance can be observed.
b. Motor learning can be observed.
c. Motor learning is the demonstration of motor skills.
d. Motor performance is permanent.

88. Which of the following behaviors is an example of an adaptive coping skill?

a. A person experiencing stress related to eating and weight gain restricts his or her food intake.
b. A person experiencing performance anxiety practices breathing techniques before a test.
c. A person who becomes easily nervous making new friends avoids social gatherings.
d. A person who experiences stress about a new health issue avoids going to the doctor.

89. In addition to a physically active lifestyle, which of the following aspects of nutrition is most closely related to maintaining body weight, as opposed to losing or gaining weight?

a. Ensuring caloric intake and expenditure match
b. Ensuring the foods you eat are nutrient-dense
c. Ensuring you limit bad fats, sugars, and sodium
d. Ensuring calories increase or decrease in time

Refer to the following for question 90:

Students in physical education participate in an annual dance-off fundraising competition with students in the dance program. The competition involves several performances which require strength and stamina. The students are practicing the dance routines for 60 minutes, five days a week. However, the teacher notices at the end of the first week that several students are jerky in their movements during the performance.

90. On which movement concept does the teacher need to focus to help students move more smoothly?

a. Force
b. Time
c. Flow
d. Levels

Constructed Response

91. Cynthia plans to introduce yoga to her physical education classes this week. She hopes to incorporate yoga poses such as downward dog and tree pose. Through these lessons, students will work on their ability to demonstrate actions such as twisting and stretching.

Based on the plans above and your knowledge of these types of movements:

- Explain the differences between locomotor and non-locomotor movement.
- Identify if Cynthia's lesson will focus on locomotor or non-locomotor movement.
- Describe a way that Cynthia could also incorporate an alternative type of movement into her lessons.

Answer Key and Explanations for Test #1

Selected Response

1. C: Researchers find a **mastery-oriented climate** includes effective learning strategies, student preferences for challenging work (A), positive attitudes about the class (B), and the belief that success comes from effort (D), all of which promote adaptive learning behaviors. They find a **performance-oriented climate** includes focusing on ability, not effort, and norm-referenced evaluation criteria (C), which promote maladaptive learning behaviors.

2. B: The best professional development not only improves a teacher's own expertise (A) and that of the teacher's colleagues (C) but both mutually as well as enabling physical education teachers to promote their own discipline. It enables teachers to improve instruction not only at the classroom level (D) but also at schoolwide and districtwide levels.

3. D: Although being in a car accident can certainly cause stress, it is not a risk factor of suicide. Risk factors include previous suicide attempts, history of mental illness, serious or chronic illness, criminal or legal problems, financial problems, substance use, and history of abuse in childhood. Although the car accident could contribute to a risk factor of suicide (e.g., causing financial problems), it is not a risk factor itself.

4. B: Skill circuit variation can aid in skill development and refinement to meet diverse learners or mixed-ability groups. All students can work on the same skills but are challenged according to their ability. For example, in a shooting circuit, beginner students can work on technique closer to the basketball goal, intermediate students can shoot mid-range, and advanced students can shoot at farther distances at the same circuit. While student choice has been shown to increase motivation, students may not necessarily choose tasks that match or improve their ability. Combining mixed-ability or pairing advanced and beginner students is appropriate in some settings, e.g., peer assessment, but advanced and beginner students can become frustrated, so progress may suffer at both ends of the ability continuum. Beginner students may also get injured by intermediate and advance students, especially during gameplay activities.

5. B: Vision is the perceptual motor ability that aids in movement detection and movement response. If Kenya is closing her eyes, that may be causing increased balance and coordination difficulty, as those sensory responses are not activated. Hearing perception is important for motor skill development but is more closely related to the body preparing to take action, for example, when hearing "go" or "start," or the sound of a thrown or caught ball.

6. D: Recently, the issue that has become the greatest challenge to kindergarten to Grade 12 (K–12) school physical education (PE) is that time in school curricula for PE classes and activities has been reduced significantly to make time for other academic classes. Inadequate resources and parental support (A); overly large class sizes and teacher burnout (B); and violence, student drug abuse, and discipline problems (C) are also challenges to K–12 PE, but these are also equal challenges to other school subjects and to education in general.

7. B: Chasing, fleeing, and dodging games help develop the movement concepts of spatial awareness, relationships with self/others/equipment, and effort. These movements also help with strategies and tactics used in individual (tennis) and team sports (basketball).

8. D: Dodging is defined as sharply changing direction, e.g., away from another player or an object. It is classified as a non-locomotor skill because it does not require running, sidestepping (sliding), jumping, or otherwise moving the body's support base or changing position. Running (A), jumping (B), and climbing (C) are all classified as locomotor skills because they do involve moving the body from point to point in space.

9. D: Body weight training (c) uses no equipment, just the student's own body weight, for resistance. Partner resistance exercises (b) also require no equipment, just two students taking turns providing and working against resistance. Free weight work (a) can use dumbbells, kettlebells, etc., of different weights, or barbells to which weights can be added and subtracted; this requires equipment, but not the number or variety included in circuit training (d), which involves completing circuits through a series of different weight machines quickly without interruption.

10. A: Kimberly needs to hear or see the skill cue to "step with the opposite foot of your throwing arm" to remind her of the movements. Practice will only work if Kimberly is practicing the correct movements. Working with a partner may or may not work, as it depends on the skill level of the partner. While all students may not master every skill, cues to help students improve should continue.

11. C: Cross-training and monitoring type and amount of food intake can aid in healthy body composition. Increasing physical activity can offset some effects of consuming excessive fat. Physical activity cannot mitigate some harmful effects of excessive fat consumption, e.g., high cholesterol. Food is needed for a healthy body and should not be avoided but should be consumed in moderation. Reading food labels aids in making informed choices about foods, but reading the labels will not establish a healthy body composition if one is consuming high-fat, low-nutrient meals. Moving more is vague, and an explicit goal that is shown to be effective is missing, such as "to move 30 to 60 minutes per day."

12. A: A muscular endurance goal requires that the muscle work for longer periods of time. Therefore, the higher the rep count, the greater the endurance. Increased soreness likely indicates that the overload principle was employed without progression to meet strength goals. Maintaining the same rep count over time does not indicate improvement effectiveness but simply maintenance. Maintenance is good for individuals who have met their fitness goals, but variation in activities ensures that the body continues to respond to exercise's physiological benefits. Increasing weight over time will gradually occur with endurance, whereas increasing weight complements a strength-building increase.

13. D: The teach-back method is an effective strategy to gauge patient understanding. It can be helpful for embedding important instructions and correcting any inaccurate information. Summarizing critical information, using visual aids, and offering multiple complementary educational materials are helpful strategies for reinforcing health education, but not necessarily for confirming comprehension.

14. D: The DECIDE model can be used to guide users through responsible decision-making. DECIDE is an acronym for define the problem (D), establish the criteria (E), consider the possible choices (C), identify the best solution (I), develop and implement the solution (D), and evaluate the solution (E).

15. D: Research proves weight-bearing exercise strengthens bones, lowering risk for osteoporosis and associated bone fractures. Exercise lowers risk for colon cancer, breast cancer, and some others, but is not proven to lower risk for every kind of cancer (A). It lowers risk for Alzheimer's-type dementia including memory loss (B), as well as depression. It lowers risk for Type 2 diabetes, not Type 1 (Type 1 has a stronger genetic component, so even physically active children can develop it; however, carefully monitored and controlled exercise helps them manage this condition).

16. B: The teacher is facilitating relationships with objects by moving over and under equipment. Forward and backward reinforce spatial awareness directions. Straight and curved support spatial awareness pathways, and strong and light are effort or force movement concepts.

17. A: Some medical conditions, such as hypertension, can be exacerbated by engaging in certain physical activities; therefore, it is important to know if participants are predisposed to or have hereditary health conditions to ensure a safe exercise environment. Musculoskeletal injuries are generally the result of overtraining, muscle overuse, awkward movements, colliding with a person or object, or are age-related, such as with osteoporosis.

18. B: The US Department of Agriculture (USDA) is the leading organization on nutrition. The Food and Drug Administration (FDA) controls what ingredients are allowed in food but does not control nutrition guidelines like the USDA does. The Environmental Protection Agency (EPA) and the Department of Transportation (DOT) do not play a role in disseminating nutritional information or any developing food-related laws or guidelines.

19. A: A chasse is a ballet step adopted in jazz and modern dance and is similar to the gallop where one foot leads and the other follows. An axel is a turn used in jazz and modern dance but consists of turning while hopping. The ball change is a transition step used in jazz that consists of transferring weight on the balls of the feet, similar to the weight transfer that occurs in the grapevine step. The drop is an intentional fall to the ground, often after performing a leap.

20. B: Discipline is important when engaging in recreational activities since there is no one to monitor activity, hold the individual accountable, or help maintain motivation as would occur under the direction of a teacher or coach. The rules for recreational activities should be researched before engagement. Goals vary among individuals, but this does not explain why discipline is important. Outcome goals, such as fun, fitness, and competition tend to be clear, and creating goals helps with motivation and discipline.

21. C: Students engage in walking, jogging, and running when engaged in orienteering. In a triathlon, fitness activities include swimming, cycling, and running or jogging. Hiking, swimming, and cycling benefit muscular and cardiovascular fitness but are not skills used in orienteering.

22. B: Students can evaluate their cardiorespiratory fitness by tracking their resting heart rate over time. As cardiorespiratory fitness increases, resting and exercise heart rates decrease. To improve cardiovascular fitness, students should work at their target heart rate zone. The talk test is a subjective measure that is used during cardiovascular activity to gauge intensity. Reflections can be used to aid in the evaluation but may include subjective and objective data. A subjective data example may include students reporting how they felt during the activity by stating something like, "I can tell that my cardiorespiratory fitness is improving because I was not out of breath." An objective data example may be students reporting their heart rate data in their journals. Regardless of the method, criteria need to be set for evaluating cardiorespiratory fitness.

23. A: FITT = Frequency, Intensity, Time, Type. How long to work out (A) = Time, which is determined by the Intensity and Type of exercise. How to ensure overload without overtraining (B), burnout, or injury = Intensity. How often to work out to ensure enough stress to make the body adapt plus allow healing through enough rest (C) = Frequency. Specific exercises to do, and whether the workout is cardio, resistance (weight), or both combined (D) = Type.

24. C: A person who avoids sharing his or her opinions or feelings is exhibiting passive communication. Using "I" statements and seeking to understand the speaker's point of view can promote understanding and compassion within both parties. Setting boundaries can establish acceptable behavior and encourage accountability.

25. C: A BMI of 18.5 to 24.9 is classified as a normal, healthy proportion of body fat to height and weight. A BMI of 18.5 or lower (a) is considered underweight, i.e., insufficient body fat. A BMI of 25.0 to 29.9 (c) is classified as overweight, i.e., excessive body fat. A BMI of 30 or higher (d) is classified as obese, i.e., extremely excessive body fat.

26. B: When participation in PE or other physical activities is impeded by student insecurities (A), this is an example of the impact of psychological factors on motor development and performance. The widespread phenomenon of playing video games to the exclusion of physical ones (B) is the best example of the impact of social factors. Poor home living conditions (C) are an example of the impact of environmental factors. Illnesses and disabilities (D) are examples of health factors.

27. D: According to the US Department of Health and Human Services (HHS) Office of Adolescent Health (OAH), on typical days teenagers get almost 40 percent of their calories from sugars and solid fats, not 30 percent (a); recreational TV watching equals or exceeds three hours for almost one-third of teens, not one-quarter (b); parental support and active siblings DO influence adolescents to become and remain active (c); and the majority of teens sleep fewer hours nightly than needed for good health (d).

28. C: Free weight exercises help improve flexibility and posture. These exercises are conducted using a full range of motion at the joints and strengthening muscles that aid in keeping the body in an upright position. Isometric exercises are those that use static positions that require muscular resistance, such as wall sits and planks, and do not allow for a repeated range of motion. Running reduces flexibility as the repetitive motion strengthens but tightens the muscles.

29. C: The teacher aims to develop tactical skills or decision-making and action skills required for effective gameplay. Psychomotor skills are actions or movements only. Transfer skills occur in invasion games but the question is specific to soccer and not invasion games generally. Affective skills would include attitudes, feelings, and values for soccer.

30. B: Characteristics of developmentally appropriate PE include that individual children are more alike than different, not vice versa (A); that individual children all go through the same developmental stages (B); that they go through these stages in the same, not varying, order (C); and that individual children develop at different, not similar, rates (D).

31. D: Differentiation is a strategy that addresses multiple abilities that exist in one class. The teacher should have activities for beginner, intermediate, and advanced students to meet all learners' needs and include extensions and remediations. Some students have mastered or exceeded the learning outcome but still need to be challenged and learn new ways of doing things.

32. C: Tidal volume, i.e., the amount of air displaced between inhaling and exhaling, increases as a short-term effect of exercise on the respiratory system, which is part of the cardiorespiratory system. Long-term effects of exercise are a lower resting heartrate (a); increased vital capacity (b), i.e., the most air one can expel from the lungs after inhaling the most air possible; and greater stroke volume (d), i.e., how much blood the heart pumps from the left ventricle per beat.

33. B: Getting adequate sleep has been shown to help manage stress as it restores and calms the body and improves concentration, decision-making, and judgment. Most sleep recommendations are 8-10 hours a night. Short naps have also been shown to have similar benefits, including strengthening the immune system and regulating blood pressure that increases during stressful events. Watching television can aid in escaping stress, but it can have an adverse effect and increase stress depending on what is viewed and the length of screen time. Drinking caffeine has been shown to increase the stress response and interfere with sleep quality. Drinking one glass of red wine has shown stress reduction benefits, but over indulgence of alcohol interferes with sleep quality and duration. Over indulgence of alcohol can also lead to alcohol dependence and alcoholism.

34. A: Cephalocaudal means literally head-to-tail. This is the pattern of physical development for human embryos, fetuses, infants, and children. Proximodistal (B) means development from the inside out, which is also a pattern of human physical growth. (These two are not mutually exclusive but concurrent.) Mediolateral (C) is not a term generally used; but *medial* means toward the midline or closer to the inside, and *lateral* means away from the midline or closer to the outside, so "mediolateral" would have a meaning similar to proximodistal. Intellectual development (D) is like cognitive development and does not refer to patterns of motor or physical development.

35. A: Knowledge of Performance (KP) is more applicable as feedback when the student is practicing a sport skill in isolation, when correct form and technique indicate success; Knowledge of Results (KR) is the more appropriate form of feedback for the student when participating in actual play, when the outcome of the game indicates success. (B) is the reverse of this. Since (A) is correct, (C) and (D) are not.

36. A: Exercise depletes the muscles' glycogen stores, so within the first 30 minutes to two hours after exercising, participants should eat or drink simple carbohydrates while muscles absorb them better. Students and others with inadequate diets may need vitamin-mineral supplements, but with balanced nutrition, these are generally unnecessary (b). Although adequate daily hydration is critical in both everyday activities and exercise, it is a myth that everybody needs eight glasses a day (c): amount of fluid loss determines amount of water needed. Vitamins do not supply energy (d); they help release chemical energy from foods.

37. C: The student should kick underneath the ball with the shoelaces and follow through to achieve maximum elevation and flight down the field. Kicking with the toe should be avoided because it increases the risk of injury and is not as easy to control due to lack of surface area. The student is correctly taking two steps while dropping the ball from waist height and leaning back.

38. C: Rhythmic activities like dance and creative movements help students learn to control their bodies. While music is often used, the primary goal is body control. Locomotor, non-locomotor, and manipulative movements are used during rhythmic activities which can aid in the performance of skills, like gymnastics or dance routines.

39. D: Coach Wheelock is demonstrating low expectations and gender stereotypes of female students despite their role as basketball athletes. He assumes that they would not be able to play with the boys. He also assumes that all boys play rough, which is another gender stereotype. Rules should be in place to ensure safety for all students. As long as the girls can play basketball in class, separating groups by gender would not be considered gender discrimination or favoritism towards the boys.

40. C: The President's Council on Physical Fitness and Sports identifies "Fundamental Building Blocks" for using PE to promote positive student development. The structure of these is that giving opportunities and access to PA for all young people enables establishing ideal contexts for engaging in PA, which in turn allows PE educators to help students attain developmental health outcomes.

41. A: The pathways used to teach locomotor movements are straight, curved, and zigzag. Moving right, left, forward, backward and diagonal are directions the body can travel and are used to teach locomotor movements, dance, and sports skills.

42. C: Ms. Jones should evaluate her instructional skill cues and other teaching practices to determine if they meet the intended outcome or if they need to change to ensure that students are proficient by the end of 8th grade. Dribbling is a skill taught in elementary(B), so students should build on those skills in grades 6, 7, and 8. After-school instruction may be beneficial (D), but it would not be the next logical step as a change in instruction needs to occur prior to this because students could potentially continue to practice poor instructional cues. While not all students will meet the outcomes, the goal is to continue to work towards these outcomes (A).

43. A: During the latest part of the sensorimotor stage, from around 18 to 24 months of age, Piaget said children develop early symbolic function when they begin using symbols to represent other things, like playing make-believe by pretending to be adults or fictional characters and using objects to represent other things or beings, for example, pretending a broom is a horse, a block is a phone, and so on. In the preoperational stage (B), children fully develop symbolic function and display more intuitive than logical thinking. Though capable of basic mental operations, they do not perform logical ones. In concrete operations (C), they begin performing logical mental operations but only concerning concrete objects or events. In formal operations (D), they begin performing mental operations that are abstract as well as logical.

44. D: The student lacks buoyancy and can fill up their lungs with air to help keep them afloat. Emptying the air in the lungs will decrease buoyancy and cause the student to sink. Drag slows down a swimmer and can be caused by wearing clothes or when the body is not in a streamlined position.

45. A: Eustress is positive or good stress. It is often short-term and motivates or energizes a person to change (e.g., learn a new skill, start a new job, move to a new place). Distress is negative stress that causes anxiety and hinders performance (e.g., interpersonal conflict, unemployment, divorce). Acute stress is short-term and generally caused by a situational stressor. Academic stress refers to distress experienced by students related to school-related internal stressors (e.g., poor study habits and time management, academic achievement expectations) and external stressors (e.g., difficult assignments or high workload, poor teaching performance by educators). Like other forms of negative stress, academic stress can result in poor motivation, academic performance, and sleep hygiene along with an increased risk of depression and anxiety.

46. D: Malnutrition is not only caused by eating too little; it is also caused by eating foods that are not nutritious, eating unbalanced diets, and not getting enough of all necessary nutrients. Thus, people can eat too much and become overweight, but if most of the calories they consume are "empty", i.e., they contain few or no vitamins, minerals, protein, healthy fats, or fiber, they can suffer malnutrition. In fact, overconsumption of refined carbohydrates that lack fiber instead of whole grains; saturated and trans fats instead of monounsaturated and polyunsaturated fats; and processed foods instead of fruits and vegetables contribute to both obesity and malnutrition. Anxiety, depression, and other emotional factors can not only disrupt sleeping and eating, but also cause high blood pressure and heart disease (A). Stress and family dysfunction can cause both emotional and physical illness (B). Air pollution is found both to aggravate and to cause asthma (C).

47. A: The teacher is demonstrating a type of formative assessment, which is used to identify student strengths and weaknesses, and provide feedback on how to improve or refine. Formative assessment is also called assessment *of* learning, whereas assessment *for* learning is summative assessment, which identifies what students have learned and comes at the end of the unit or lesson. Assessment *as* learning are self-assessments that students engage in to monitor their own progress and make changes accordingly, which aid in deepening understanding of the tasks.

48. D: Alcohol, cocaine, marijuana, and other substances temporarily can reduce inhibitions so that students who are usually shy or introverted behave more sociably around peers. When students see substance use as a solution to being socially awkward and unpopular, they repeat it, which can lead to addiction. Conversely, students who were normally extroverted often withdraw socially when they become addicted to substances. Students who normally demonstrate self-control often behave more impulsively under the influence of substances. While some substances can result in short-term improvements in focus, substance abuse does not typically result in long-term, sustained improvement.

49. D: The Society for Health and Physical Educators (SHAPE) America sets the national K-12 and physical education teacher education standards. The Council for the Accreditation of Educator Preparation (CAEP) is responsible for accreditation of physical education teacher education programs and working closely with SHAPE America. GOPHER is the largest equipment supplier for physical education and has partnered with SHAPE America. The former National Association of Sport and Physical Education (NASPE) is now SHAPE after combining with the American Alliance for Health, Physical Education, Recreation and Dance.

50. B: An interest group is comprised of individuals with similar goals who are participating voluntarily. Typically, they share a common mission and actively work toward increasing awareness and acceptance of their interest among others. Friendship groups are comprised of individuals who are bonded by a shared experience. Task and functional groups include individuals who work together to achieve a common task or goal.

51. D: Sixty minutes every day is the recommended amount of moderate to vigorous physical activity for all K-12 students; however, it is recommended that students in elementary grades engage in 15-minute bouts of continuous activities several times a day to accumulate the 60-minute recommendation. Early adolescents are encouraged to engage in at least 20-minute bouts. Older adolescents or high school-aged students are encouraged to engage in continuous physical activity from 20- to 60-minute bouts each day.

52. B: PE teachers should design, choose, modify, and sequence game activities not simply to keep students busy (a) or prevent misbehavior (c). While they should ensure these activities promote maximum student enjoyment, this should not be the only purpose without any learning goals (d). Rather, they should aim for activities to promote student fitness, skill improvement, practice in sport-specific skills, AND enjoyment (b).

53. C: Babies typically can play "pattycake" between 7–15 months of age, at an average age of around 9 months. They typically can pull up to stand between 9–12 months, at an average age of around 8 months. They typically develop the pincer grasp (D) for picking up small objects between 9–12 months. Children with normal development typically can jump in place (C) between 17–30 months of age, at an average age of around 23½ months, i.e., almost two years old.

54. C: Dribbling a soccer ball is on the upper end of the skill progression continuum, as it combines a locomotor movement with an object (a manipulative skill) and is one of the most difficult fundamental movement skills. Skipping, running, and jumping are basic locomotor or fundamental movements.

55. D: PE classes must have a working cell phone or other communication device, regardless whether the equipment installation is in the school or elsewhere (a); the same applies to having a fully stocked, easily accessible first aid kit (b). Climbing ropes must also be compatible with the planned climbing activity and the belay device selected; these are NOT all compatible (c). Equipment must be manufactured specifically for the activity planned, and meet uniform standards (d).

56. C: Levels of responsibility defining positive youth development goals incorporate self-management skills, including **self-control**, exemplified by respecting others' feeling and rights (a) and approaching conflict resolution democratically (d); **self-motivation**, shown in trying out new tasks and persistence on tasks (b) and exemplifying effort; and **self-direction**, exemplified by working independently, setting goals progressively (c), and resisting peer pressure.

57. B: The size of the heart increases from consistent participation in cardiovascular activities. The body becomes more reliant on glucose to faster fuel the working muscles. Blood volume also increases as a result of the heart's strengthening which allows for more blood to circulate. Lactic acid removal is more efficient, allowing for a faster recovery.

58. D: Destroying the victim's property is an example of domestic abusers' typical tactics of intimidation, which they use to frighten victims into submission by indicating the violent consequences they will suffer if they do not comply with the abuser. Examples of isolation include cutting their victims off from contact with family and friends to make the victims dependent on the abusers. Examples of humiliation include making victims feel worthless and undermining their self-esteem by shaming them both in private and public. Examples of denying include saying the abuse did not occur or that it didn't happen the way the victim remembers.

59. D: When hiring a personal trainer, the student should check to see if the personal trainer is certified, the certification agency, and if the certification is current as personal training certifications require cognitive knowledge and practical application of skills. A college degree is not required to become a certified personal trainer and does not guarantee that the trainer has knowledge of personal training concepts and skills. However, a college degree in a physical activity field, e.g., physical education, kinesiology, or exercise and sport science, is required for the more reputable personal training certification agencies. Experience in body building or fitness training and referrals help with advertising and marketing but do not indicate the level of knowledge that the trainer has.

60. D: Small-sided lacrosse games are the next logical step to test skills in isolation within a modified version of a full lacrosse game. Small-sided games allow students more opportunities to respond to develop sports-specific skills. Offensive and defensive skills can be taught during small-sided games but are more effective when students can first perform the basic skills. Game observation and analysis can help identify various aspects of gameplay. However, students must have many opportunities to engage in specific activities for them to improve in the sport.

61. C: Four major principles of motor development are: children are NOT miniature adults (A); among children, boys and girls are more similar than different (B); children get good things by earning them (C); and nobody, and no body, is perfect (D). (A), (B), and (D) each contradict one of these principles; (C) reflects one of them more accurately than the others.

62. A: According to the principle of available force, movement speed and available force have an inverse relationship; i.e., as one increases, the other decreases; thus (C) is incorrect. This principle explains, in part, similarities among sports that the student in the question recognizes: taking off too fast in the broad jump can reduce force, hence distance (A); NOT swinging too fast gets better results in golf (B); and movement speed has a limit in the shot put (D).

63. B: The PE teacher should first check the scene for safety. Next, she would check the spectator for signs of consciousness, e.g., talking, breathing, and pulse. If there is no breathing, the PE teacher would identify and instruct someone to call 911 and include the assessment. If there is an AED available, that request would also be made followed by CPR until the AED arrives, medical personnel arrive, and/or the PE teacher is too tired to continue performing CPR correctly.

64. B: A teacher has no professional, legal, or ethical responsibility to share student questions about contraception with a parent or caregiver. Permission slips offer parents the opportunity to opt out of school-led sensitive education topics. Teachers are mandatory reporters, which means that they are required to report any form of abuse.

65. C: Sliding can be avoided by discussing personal values and visions or goals for the relationship, exploring the pros and cons, logistics, and possible outcomes of a potential decision, and establishing healthy boundaries and conflict resolution strategies. Although decision-making should be shared, both parties should be active and present for each decision. This can prevent miscommunication of wants, needs, and values as well as potential conflict.

66. D: Getting rest and eating a meal with carbohydrates will help students prepare for a cross country meet as both contribute to the athlete having more energy and reduced fatigue. Energy from carbohydrates is easier and faster to recruit than energy from fats. The race would be over before fat energy could be used. Rest also allows the body to recover from the muscular stress that occurs during exercise. A practice run one day prior may be disadvantageous as the body will likely experience a faster fatigue rate which can negatively affect performance. A walk-through of the course is recommended to familiarize the runners with the course.

67. C: Inline skates position all wheels in a straight line one wheel wide, whereas quad (traditional) skates position two front and two back wheels, each side by side, creating four (quad) contact points. However, this is not the only difference (a). Skaters find quad skates more maneuverable, not inline (b). Most skaters find inline skates to be faster, and these skates can also make it easier for skaters to avoid being stopped by small obstacles on rough surfaces (c). Although many prefer inline skates outdoors and quad skates indoors, just as many use either or both types in either or both settings (d).

68. A: Muscular endurance is the bridge between muscular strength and cardiovascular endurance. In order to exercise long enough to condition the cardiovascular system to a fit level, one must first have or develop enough muscular endurance. Muscular strength alone determines how much force the muscles can exert at one time, but muscular endurance determines how long the muscles can work.

69. C: The next step will be to choose a doctor from her list. This is the fifth step in the seven-step decision-making process. Step one is to identify the decision that is to be made. In this case, that is the need for a doctor. Step two is to gather relevant information. For this scenario, Valerie would need to consider her needs, like location and what she is looking for in a provider. Step three is to identify alternatives; Valerie did this by compiling a list of multiple approved doctors. Step four, weighing evidence, was completed when Valerie read the reviews of doctors online. Step five, choosing among alternatives, will occur when she selects a doctor from her list. Step six is called taking action. This is when she will contact and see the doctor she chose. The final step is to review her decision. She will assess her overall experience with the doctor and move forward based on how she feels.

70. B: Bodyweight exercises are recommended for beginning students in weight training. Bodyweight exercises reduce the risk of injury and teach students how to move the body for physiological adaptations. After bodyweight exercises, light weights, including dumbbells, are introduced with gradual increases in weight. Students are often directed to select a light weight and perform a few reps and, if too easy, select a heavier weight in small increments until the last two or three reps in an 8-to-15-rep count are challenging. This can be used to conduct a predicted one-repetition max test by using predicted one-rep max calculators. The one-repetition max strength test is not appropriate for physical education as lifting the heaviest amount possible in one-rep increases injury risk. Alternating between light and heavy weight is a training method for muscular strength and endurance goals but is not employed with beginners.

71. C: Students benefit from teamwork in sports by learning important social skills for life, like communicating and cooperating with others (A); socializing actively instead of playing video games, watching TV, etc. (B); and learning the value of commitment, dedication (D), and hard work through competing together as a group. However, it is also important for students to realize that in sports, winning should not always be the only goal above everything else (C).

72. D: Avoidant attachment style typically occurs when a child experiences distant or unavailable caregivers. His or her strong sense of independence and self-sufficiency emerges as he or she learns to self-soothe, yet he or she is often unable to form deep relationships with others when he or she is older. Anxious attachment occurs when caregivers are inconsistent, which causes the child to develop confusion and anxiety. Those with anxious attachment are overly attentive to their partners and constantly seek their approval. Disorganized attachment develops when a child experiences trauma or abuse. Individuals with disorganized attachment long for closeness and intimacy, yet they often push others away. Those with secure attachment experience appropriate care and support and will usually cultivate healthy relationships.

73. C: A universal school-based violence prevention program delivers lessons and activities aimed at reducing violence and classroom disruption among students (e.g., social and anger management skills, problem-solving and conflict resolution, counseling). Programs are implemented schoolwide rather than on an individual level for identified students. Additional components like collaborative classroom activities, parental and community involvement, and school environment modifications can generate a stronger impact. There is little to no evidence that increasing the security presence or implementing punitive policies and approaches (e.g., zero-tolerance, suspension, expulsion, loss of privileges) reduce violent incidents in schools. In fact, these approaches can lead to poor academic performance and engagement, along with an increased risk of legal consequences or exposure to violence. Students that are not white, able-bodied, heterosexual, cisgender, or whose first language is not English are also disproportionately impacted by punitive policies. Behavioral risk assessments are used to prevent school violence by evaluating the severity and seriousness of a student's threat of violence. Behavioral risk assessments can be an effective preventative intervention if identified students are given mental health, safety planning, and conflict resolution services. Disciplinary action should be limited when implementing behavioral risk assessments as it may incite violence or aggression.

74. A: A child with Attention Deficit Hyperactivity Disorder (ADHD) who becomes exhausted from engaging in excessive physical activity is an example of an emotional (and behavioral) condition that can affect levels of physical activity and fitness. A child with depression who avoids physical activity is also an example of this. The need to monitor a child with asthma for breathing problems during exercise (B) is an example of how a physical factor can affect physical activity and fitness levels, as are the need to monitor the exercise of a child with diabetes and coordinate it with the child's diet (C), and a physically disabled child's need for adaptive equipment (and/or alternative instructional methods) to participate in physical activities (D).

75. B: Childhood obesity has been instrumental in the shift from team sports to health-related fitness in physical education programs. Childhood obesity is attributed to sedentary lifestyles and low-quality, high-fat foods. Technology (e.g., heart rate monitors, pedometers, activity trackers, fitness and nutrition apps) is a trend that has enhanced the tracking and measurement of health-related fitness outcomes. Health-related fitness activities help prepare students for life-long activities that are conducted during adulthood, which is an unchanged goal of the education process. Health promotion is the current focus as a result of childhood obesity and physical inactivity.

76. B: Elementary is the most appropriate school level to teach movement education as it is the foundation for the fundamental movements (locomotor and non-locomotor), movement concepts (spatial awareness, relationships, and effort), and the three domains of learning (psychomotor, cognitive, and affective). These foundational skills and concepts aid in progressive, mature movements taught in middle and high school needed for individual and team sports, as well as fitness activities. Some pre-kindergarten programs are included in elementary school physical education programs, while others are offered at daycare centers.

77. D: In stage 1 of motor learning, babies and toddlers develop beyond simple reflexive movements (e.g., rooting, sucking, startling, Babinski, Moro, palmar, plantar) to fundamental purposeful movements like sitting, crawling, standing, and walking. In stage 2, young children develop more complex motor patterns (B), like running, climbing, jumping, balancing, catching, and throwing. In stage 3, older children develop greater automaticity and fluidity in performing the stage 2 motor patterns (C) while learning more specific movement skills. In stage 4, adolescents master specialized movements while ability, motivation, and practice influence continuing general and specific motor skills development (D).

78. C: This scenario is an example of tolerance. Omar's parents tolerate his decision even though it is different than what they want. Omar's parents would have demonstrated acceptance if they affirmed his decision without trying to dissuade him. Neither Omar nor his parents attempted to understand each other's perspectives or empathize.

79. B: Motive force is how much a lever can move an object; resistive force is how much resistance the object has against being moved by the lever. In the MA ratio, if the quotient is more than 1, resistive force is greater than motive force, not less (d). If the quotient is less than 1, motive force exceeds resistive force, not vice versa (a). If the quotient equals 1, there is NO advantage (c).

80. B: First aid procedures include RICE (rest, ice, compression, and elevation) to reduce inflammation. Immobilization restricts movement and further damage. Moving or mobilization (A) may cause more damage. Heat (C) is used for long-term musculoskeletal injuries but for new injuries or when in doubt, use ice. Heat can increase swelling and inflammation of new injuries. Calling 911 (D) is for life-threatening injuries. Sprains heal in time. Severe sprains and follow-up visits tend to occur with a primary care or orthopedic doctor.

81. A: A dynamic warm-up is a safe practice for dance and other physical activities to prepare the body for vigorous work and prevent injury. Static movements or stationary stretching should occur at the end of the activity as stretching a cold muscle increases the risks of muscle tears and blood pools to the muscle stretched instead of throughout the body to all muscles used. Wearing loose clothing may be more comfortable but generally is not considered a safety precaution. Yoga stretches and poses consist of many static movements or stretches held for long periods, which restricts blood flow from circulation to all the muscles.

82. B: Body composition is the individual body's ratio of lean body mass to body fat. It depends most on the other four components, i.e., flexibility (a), cardiovascular endurance (c), muscular strength (d), and muscular endurance, because improving these will naturally improve the body composition after consistent fitness conditioning over time.

83. C: The appropriate training schedule for a midfielder in soccer is interval training with the Fartlek method of switching between random speeds consisting of short sprints, running downfield, walking, and jogging. These are helpful because movements in soccer can vary drastically. Long duration training is more appropriate for endurance activities including cross country and cycling. Short duration training is more appropriate for short or explosive activities, e.g., the 100-meter sprint and jumping. Duration training is specific to the game or position rather than the player.

84. A: Assuming that Tom will stop any unwanted sexual advances based on Louisa's nonverbal cues is the least effective strategy. Effective refusal skills include making excuses, making a joke, saying "no," redirecting the conversation, proposing alternative activities, and physically leaving the situation.

85. D: Researchers have observed consistent gender differences in preschool physical and motor development; however, they also observe that in spite of these differences, the physical and motor development of preschoolers is more similar than different between genders. In general, the differences are not significant enough to place any emphasis on motor development differences between preschool boys and girls. Some known differences, however, include that preschool boys are more muscular than preschool girls, but preschool girls are more physically mature than preschool boys (A). While preschool boys exhibit more strength in large-muscle, gross-motor skills, preschool girls exhibit more coordination in large-muscle, gross-motor skills (B and C). Additionally, preschool girls are superior to preschool boys in fine-motor skills as well as gross-motor coordination (C).

86. B: Angular momentum occurs during the roll portion of the forward roll, which is any rotating body or object around an axis where inertia, or resistant force, decreases given the body's ball-shape. Inertia is evident at the end of the forward roll or when the roll stops. The push-off is the force applied at the start of the roll. The angle of release is the biomechanical principle applied to projectiles or airborne objects like a thrown ball.

87. A: Motor performance can be observed, but motor learning cannot. Observing motor performance over time can aid in the determination of motor learning. Motor learning is permanent, e.g., riding a bicycle; however, motor performance changes based on the environment, such as lack of rest or facing a tough defender.

88. B: Adaptive coping skills are behaviors that help a person manage or relieve stress in a healthy way (e.g., meditation, mindfulness, breathing, exercise, problem-solving). Maladaptive coping strategies are negative behaviors that relieve immediate stress but worsen stress overall. Examples include avoidance or procrastination, substance use, and self-harm.

89. A: Taking in and expending the same amount of calories is most closely related to weight maintenance. Eating nutrient-dense foods (b) and limiting saturated and trans fats, sugars, and salt (c) are more related to ensuring you meet your caloric needs while still providing adequate quantity and quality of nutrients. Increasing or decreasing calories taken in over time (d) is related to gaining or losing weight, not maintaining it.

90. C: The teacher needs to focus on teaching students the concept of flow, which is the contrast between smooth and jerky movements. Force focuses on the amount of effort or intensity of a movement. Time is the rate or speed of a given activity, which can aid in teaching flow by asking students to move at a slow pace, but time is not the concept that needs clarification. The term *levels* addresses the different heights at which a movement is performed.

Constructed Response

91. This is the rubric used to score constructed-response questions on the CSET.

Purpose	The extent to which the response addresses the constructed-response assignment's charge in relation to relevant CSET content specifications or subject matter requirements.
Subject Matter Knowledge	Application of accurate subject matter knowledge as described in the relevant CSET content specifications or subject matter requirements.
Support	The appropriateness and quality of the supporting evidence in relation to relevant CSET content specifications or subject matter requirements.

Score Point	Score Point Description
3	**The "3" response reflects command of the relevant knowledge and skills as defined in the CSET content specifications or subject matter requirements.** • The purpose of the assignment is fully achieved. • There is an accurate application of relevant content specifications or subject matter requirements. • There is appropriate and specific relevant supporting evidence.
2	**The "2" response reflects general command of the relevant knowledge and skills as defined in the CSET content specifications or subject matter requirements.** • The purpose of the assignment is largely achieved. • There is a largely accurate application of relevant content specifications or subject matter requirements. • There is acceptable relevant supporting evidence.
1	**The "1" response reflects limited or no command of the relevant knowledge and skills as defined in the CSET content specifications or subject matter requirements.** • The purpose of the assignment is only partially or not achieved. • There is limited or no application of relevant content specifications or subject matter requirements. • There is little or no relevant supporting evidence.
U	**The "U" (unscorable) is assigned to a response that is unrelated to the assignment, illegible, primarily in a language other than English, or does not contain a sufficient amount of original work to score.**
B	**The "B" (blank) is assigned to a response that is blank.**

Practice Test #2

Selected Response

1. Students and others who are obese, or are overweight and have two or more other risk factors, can decrease their risk of developing related diseases by losing how much of their existing body weight?

a. 5-10 percent
b. 15-20 percent
c. 25-30 percent
d. 35-40 percent

2. PE curriculum can be modified to enable participation by students with special needs in the areas of directions, rules, equipment, and environment. Which choice reflects adaptations in the area of rules?

a. Lowering the basketball hoop
b. Installing padding, hand holds
c. Removing time requirements
d. Giving a student oral prompts

3. A third grader broke down and had a temper tantrum after having a series of unsuccessful forward rolls. Which of the following factors might be impeding the student's physical development?

a. emotional knowledge
b. emotional self-regulation
c. self-efficacy
d. self-esteem

4. Katherine wants to train her shoulders and neck for swim season. Which of the following exercises will meet Katherine's needs?

a. Lateral deltoid raises and shrugs
b. Shoulder curls and deltoid raises
c. Deltoid curls and shrugs
d. Anterior and rear deltoid raises

5. Which of the following exercises best work the trunk and quadriceps?

a. Curl-ups and deadlifts
b. Knee lifts and seated rows
c. Planks and squats
d. Twists and leg curls

6. Which of the following best describes the relationship between ability and skill for motor performance?

a. Abilities are genetic characteristics that are the same for all.
b. Abilities are learned traits that promote skill development.
c. Abilities are genetic characteristics that impact one's ability to learn a motor skill.
d. Individuals with low ability cannot improve their motor skills.

7. Which of the following is a solution to address multiple classes in limited gym space?

a. Team teaching
b. Rotating court space every 10-minutes
c. Utilizing outdoor spaces
d. Reducing course offerings

8. Which of the following is an example of metabolic syndrome related to sedentary lifestyles?

a. Heart disease and overactive thyroid
b. High cholesterol, hypertension, and obesity
c. Hypokinetic disease and physical inactivity
d. Obesity, low blood glucose, and diabetes

9. After tracking his teaching behaviors, Mr. Green realized that taking attendance for 40 students takes up a lot of time, which reduces student engagement. How might Mr. Green alter his attendance taking method to increase the opportunities for students to respond?

a. set a time-limit to take attendance
b. practice taking attendance faster
c. take attendance during the warm-up
d. take attendance in squad lines

10. In abusive relationships, which of these is most commonly the case?

a. When an abuser apologizes and acts normal, he or she is genuinely sorry and intends to try to change.
b. When an abuser apologizes and acts normal, he or she is manipulating the victim and will abuse again.
c. When an abuser apologizes rather than blaming the victim, this is a sign the victim can believe it.
d. When an abuser apologizes rather than blaming the victim, he or she is unlikely to repeat the abuse.

11. Use the DECIDE model to respond to the following question: Yeslia is the supervisor of four staff members. She notices that one of her employees has been less productive the past few weeks. The employee's performance has begun affecting the other employees she manages. What is the most appropriate first step?

a. Meet with the employee to brainstorm strategies for improving his or her productivity.
b. Establish the criteria that Yeslia will use to assess her employee's productivity.
c. Define any challenges or stressors that impact the employee's productivity.
d. Implement biweekly check-ins to ensure that the employee stays on track.

12. Among the following, which is recommended as a healthy way of approaching conflict?

a. Seeing mutual benefits in facing conflict directly
b. Expressing anger emotionally to enable venting
c. Avoiding conflict to prevent negative outcomes
d. Standing firm without compromising one's view

13. Students in grades 9-12 should be able to do which of these with manipulative motor skills?

a. Refining and applying complex manipulative skills in lead-up games
b. Creating advanced movement skills and demonstrating using them
c. Demonstrating progress toward more manipulative skill complexity
d. Applying basic and advanced skills to sports, dance, and gymnastics

Refer to the following for question 14:

Research shows that exercise lowers the risk of high blood pressure, stroke, and heart disease. In particular, aerobic exercise has been proven to protect the cardiovascular system.

14. Which intensity of aerobic exercise provides the greatest protection against coronary heart disease specifically?

a. Mild intensity
b. Vigorous intensity
c. Moderate intensity
d. Any level of intensity

15. Recognizing and understanding the significance of regular physical activity to healthy lifestyles is an objective most appropriate to which grade levels in public schools?

a. Grades EC-K
b. Grades K-2
c. Grades 3-5
d. Grades 6-12

16. Divers and skaters can control the speed of their turns through the length of the rotation radius around the center of gravity. Relative to this biomechanical principle, which choice is true?

a. The body turns less slowly with arms extended.
b. The body turns most slowly in the pike position.
c. The body turns most slowly in full tuck position.
d. The body turns most slowly in lay-out position.

17. Regarding the relationship of body awareness, motor skills development, perceptual skills development, and other learning in school, which statement is correct?

a. Perceptual skill development leads to body awareness and motor development.
b. The development of fine motor skills leads to development of gross motor skills.
c. Perceptual skills develop out of good motor skills, which rely on body awareness.
d. Perceptual skills, but not motor skills, help in reading, writing, and other learning.

18. Which of the following best describes the environments for open vs. closed motor skills?

a. A tennis match vs. a basketball game
b. A basketball game vs. a round of golf
c. A round of golf vs. a tennis match
d. A gymnastics routine vs. a tennis match

19. School-based health clinics provide each of the following health services EXCEPT:

a. WIC enrollment
b. Behavioral health care referrals
c. Vaccinations
d. Sexual health education

20. Which of the following is correct regarding principles of aerobic exercise?

a. Aerobic exercise involves small muscle groups.
b. Aerobic exercise entails continuous movement.
c. Aerobic exercise will firm and tone the muscles.
d. Aerobic exercise burns fat only at low intensity.

21. Spectators boo when a female golfer takes her stroke at a mixed-gender tournament. Which of the following behaviors are the spectators engaging in?

a. taunting
b. poor etiquette
c. breaking the rules
d. sexism

22. Which of the following strategies is helpful in reducing student conflict?

a. Modeling expected behaviors
b. Using peer mediation
c. Separating the students with conflict
d. Calling the parents

23. The teacher begins to incorporate movement concepts with basic locomotor and non-locomotor movements during the creative movement unit. Which of the following best describes the rationale behind this approach?

a. To accommodate multiple abilities
b. To keep students interested
c. To make movements more aesthetic
d. To illustrate dance as an art form

24. A PE teacher or coach responds to different student learning styles when teaching new movement or sport skills. Which of these instructional strategies would best help a student with a mainly verbal learning style?

a. The teacher or coach gives a demonstration of the skill to imitate.
b. The teacher or coach adds a diagram of the skill to demonstration.
c. The teacher or coach guides students through demonstrated skills.
d. The teacher or coach explains the skill aloud during demonstration.

25. Of the following, which accurately reports research findings related to how physical fitness affects academic achievement?

a. Cardiovascular fitness and a healthy body mass index (BMI) correlate positively with test scores in achievement
b. More physically fit children react more quickly but not necessarily more accurately.
c. Children burn more calories during active gaming than teacher-led fitness activities.
d. Intense exercise is followed by a significant temporary decline in cognitive function.

26. In conjunction with individual therapy and medication, which of the following strategies is most effective at reducing hospital readmission and relapses in symptoms and improving overall social functioning in individuals with schizophrenia?

a. Electroconvulsive therapy
b. Supported employment
c. Supportive family therapy
d. Group psychotherapy

27. What is a result of regular and substantial alcohol use?

a. It impairs judgment over the long term but not in the short term.
b. It distorts the perceptions but not the senses of vision or hearing.
c. It damages both the cardiovascular and central nervous systems.
d. It causes liver damage but not impotence or stomach disorders.

28. For students in the sixth grade, which of these is the best example of the competency of demonstrating mature form in manipulative skills?

a. Combining locomotor and non-locomotor skills, changing pace, level, direction in a 1-minute dance
b. Dribbling a basketball, circumventing stationary objects, using both the right hand and the left hand
c. Throwing a softball to different distances by using different amounts of force and varied trajectories
d. Keeping a log of softball practice throws at a target, contrasting successes from first to last attempts

29. In three stages of motor learning, which of these is characteristic of the associative stage?

a. Understanding an activity's goal and nature
b. Making attempts that include major errors
c. Making fewer and more consistent errors
d. Effortless automaticity in performance

30. In a public school's PE risk management and emergency procedure plans, which is typically among the provisions?

a. If any students are injured, the school nurse offers the initial first aid.
b. All physical educators carry emergency first aid kits during PE classes.
c. Not all physical educators need have current first aid and CPR certificates.
d. PE teachers may not know which students lack treatment permission.

31. Which kinds of objects are most suitable for an activity meant to support development of spatial awareness?

a. A balance beam or a vault horse
b. Several balls with different sizes
c. Different sizes of boxes or hoops
d. A gymnasium or big empty room

32. Which of the following best describes the purpose of the Presidential Youth Fitness and FitnessGram® programs?

a. To assess health-related fitness
b. To assess skill-related fitness
c. To assess health- and skill-related fitness
d. To assess dynamic fitness and sports skills

Refer to the following for question 33:

For a unit on baseball, students are learning how to make a proper overhand throw. The teacher explains that the overhand throw consists of a wind up, step, rotation, and follow through. She sets up a target for students to throw their ball toward. After several rounds of unsuccessful overhand throws for some students, the teacher moves the targets closer to them. However, these students were still unable to successfully hit their target.

33. Which of the following best describes the fundamental skill category for the overhand throw?

a. Locomotor movement
b. Non-locomotor movement
c. Manipulative movement
d. Weight transfer movement

34. Which of the following is a key responsibility of the Red Cross?

a. Providing heavy rescue and assisting with evacuations during natural disasters
b. Overseeing the manufacturing of supplements to ensure they are safe for consumption
c. Providing health care services and basic needs to communities recovering from crisis
d. Traveling abroad to provide healthcare in developing countries

35. What has research discovered about the adolescent decision-making process?

a. Conformity with parental or peer norms is unrelated to teen decision making.
b. Demographic rather than family or personal variables influence teen decisions.
c. Adolescents tend to be oriented toward the future regarding long-term goals.
d. Real-life practice is necessary for teens to transfer cognitive skills to decisions.

36. Intimate partner violence (IPV) refers to abuse that occurs within an intimate or romantic relationship (e.g., physical violence, sexual violence, stalking, aggression). Which of the following is NOT generally considered a risk factor for IPV?

a. Witnessing IPV between parents during childhood
b. Living in impoverished communities
c. High self-esteem
d. Prior history of victimization

37. Which of the following is an acute response to aerobic exercise?

a. lower resting heart rate
b. increase in ventilation
c. constant cardiac output
d. decrease in stroke volume

38. Of the following, which statement is MOST accurate about common unhealthy reactions to stress?

a. People under stress are more likely to feel physical pain than to quit smoking, drinking, or drugs.
b. People under stress are more likely to overeat and gain weight than skip eating and lose weight.
c. People under stress are more likely to display episodes of anger or temper than episodes of crying.
d. People under stress are more likely to experience symptoms of anxiety than those of depression.

39. Which of these facts about smoking is LEAST likely to discourage a 14-year-old boy from taking up the habit?

a. Smokers are ten times more likely to die of lung cancer than nonsmokers.
b. Smoking is a very expensive habit.
c. Many girls won't date a boy who smokes.
d. Smoking can seriously impair athletic performance.

40. Which of the following statements is most accurate about the role of self-assessment in developing physical fitness and lifelong participation in physical activity?

a. Self-assessment should not be required since students lack the training.
b. Self-assessment encourages reflection, which interferes with execution.
c. Self-assessment enables students to determine their current skill levels.
d. Self-assessment causes loss of control over the developmental process.

41. Which of the following strategies increases instructional time?

a. Preparing equipment ahead of time
b. Observing students to look for fatigue
c. Wearing a watch
d. Adhering to the bell schedule

42. The CDC suggests six strategies to prevent adverse childhood experiences (ACEs). Implementing family-friendly work policies is an example of which strategy?

a. Ensuring a strong start for children
b. Connecting youth to caring adults and activities
c. Strengthening economic supports to families
d. Intervening to lessen immediate and long-term harm

43. Where should a sprinter's center of gravity be to accelerate fastest out of the starting block?

a. It should be as high as possible.
b. It should be as low as possible.
c. It should be right in the middle.
d. It should be a full upright body.

44. Which of the following descriptions is most applicable to learning standards for PE students in grades 9-12?

a. Students show the ability to explore fundamental locomotor and non-locomotor skills.
b. Students are capable of demonstrating the mature forms in locomotor and non-locomotor skills.
c. Students can apply the mature forms of motor skills in specialized sports, dance, and gymnastics.
d. Students use locomotor, non-locomotor, manipulative skills in sports, dance, and gymnastics activities.

45. Which of the following best contrasts perceptual motor abilities and physical proficiency abilities?

a. Muscular endurance and muscular strength
b. Reaction time and control precision
c. Reaction time and muscular strength
d. Control precision and finger dexterity

46. The President's Council on Physical Fitness and Sports identifies personal development benefits of PE as well as physiological health benefits. The former include which of the following as social and psychological life skills rather than improved developmental outcomes?

a. Showing self-confidence
b. Showing peer resistance
c. Showing self-regulation
d. Showing perseverance

47. Concerning the impacts of various resources on student physical education (PE) outcomes, what has research shown?

a. Class size and student–teacher ratio correlate inversely with activity levels, time, safety, and learning.
b. Students receive a higher quantity and quality of PE from teachers who also teach different subjects.
c. Student physical activity is the same whether PE curriculum is based on educational standards or not.
d. PE facilities and equipment are valuable resources but do not change the amount of student activity.

48. Which of the following is the dominant movement concept when performing a leap?

a. Rhythm
b. Force
c. Time
d. Levels

49. Which of the following best describes the model used in physical education that incorporates biomechanics and Physics during the throwing unit?

a. physical education and sport science
b. integrated physical education
c. exercise and sport science
d. kinesiology

50. Which of the following is a physiological benefit of exercise that helps manage stress responses?

a. it improves mood
b. it enhances positive thoughts
c. it lowers the release of cortisol
d. it increases confidence

51. A student is experiencing stress related to an upcoming exam. Which of the following is a poor coping strategy to alleviate stress?

a. Relaxing test performance expectations
b. Practicing meditation and breathing techniques
c. Reaching out to the teacher before the exam for extra help
d. Eliminating study breaks until the student gets all of his or her study guide questions correct

52. During the spatial awareness unit, Jason could not identify the small movements essential in large gross motor activities. Which of the following perceptual-motor skills is difficult for Jason?

a. Fine motor discrimination
b. Auditory discrimination
c. Visual discrimination
d. Kinesthetic discrimination

53. Daniel received doctor's orders to strengthen his lower back before engaging in any other activities. Which of the following exercises will help him get stronger in the lower back?

a. lat pulls
b. one-arm rows
c. seated rows
d. trunk lifts

54. James' heels lift during the down phase of his squat. Which of the following identifies the issue and an exercise to help James keep his heels on the floor?

a. lack of dorsiflexion; toe raises and drops
b. lack of hip flexibility; deadlifts
c. lack of plantar extension; heel raises
d. lack of knee strength; lunges

55. A person with a/an ____________ communication style effectively and respectfully expresses his or her wants, needs, and emotions and considers the needs of others.

a. assertive
b. aggressive
c. passive
d. passive-aggressive

Refer to the following for question 56:

High school students in a physical education class are beginning an outdoor unit on tennis. During the first session, the teacher notices that some students are struggling to get the ball over the net during the forehand stroke. Later on in the week, the teacher notices that one student, Ari, is constantly having her tennis ball land beyond the baseline (out of bounds or longer) during her tennis forehand.

56. What strategy will help Ari keep the ball in-bound?

a. Adding topspin
b. Reducing the power at the point of contact
c. Increasing the speed of the racket
d. Bringing the striking arm closer to the body

57. Which of the following strategies fosters teamwork?

a. Having team captains
b. Goal setting
c. Meeting with players individually
d. Watching videos of gameplay

58. Which of the following websites would be the LEAST reliable for finding health-related information?

a. www.health.harvard.edu
b. www.cdc.gov
c. www.mayoclinic.org
d. www.tuftsuniversity.biz

59. Which of the following is an example of a psychological approach that aims to develop intrinsic student motivation in physical education?

a. Self-determination theory
b. Behaviorism theory
c. Social theory
d. Constructivism theory

60. Jack is not following through on his overhand throw. Which feedback type would likely be the most effective for skill improvement?

a. Verbal feedback
b. Video analysis and verbal feedback
c. Written feedback
d. Verbal and written feedback

61. A coach realizes that a player who fatigued early during the soccer game did not perform the pre-season workouts. Which of the following is an effective discipline strategy?

a. Having the player run laps
b. Having the player perform push-ups
c. Having the player set goals
d. Having the player sit out the next game

62. Which of the following best explains the rationale behind physical education promoting physical activity over the lifespan?

a. Lowers the risk of heart disease
b. Increases blood pressure
c. Responsible for muscle atrophy
d. Decreases endorphins

63. Which of the following is the best training program to improve muscular endurance?

a. High weight, low reps
b. High weight, high reps
c. Low weight, low reps
d. Low weight, high reps

64. What type of communication might a person use to reinforce messages and information conveyed in his or her casual speech?

a. Verbal communication
b. Written communication
c. Visual communication
d. Nonverbal communication

65. A few students have bent legs during the cartwheel but have the flexibility to do so. Which of the following may help students improve their cartwheels?

a. observations
b. skill cues
c. yoga
d. videos

66. Which of the following is a defensive running pattern common in dual and team sports?

a. high level
b. zigzags
c. transitions
d. curves

67. The teacher instructs students to dance freely in their coned-off areas. Which of the following spatial awareness concepts is the focus?

a. personal space
b. general space
c. varying space
d. non-locomotor space

68. During what stage of motor development does talent begin to play a role?

a. Stage 1
b. Stage 2
c. Stage 3
d. Stage 4

69. Which of the following is a strategy used for refinement of manipulative skills?

a. tag games
b. increased opportunities to respond
c. leading and following a peer
d. choice of manipulative skill

70. When planning for developmentally appropriate instruction, which of the following needs consideration?

a. students' sex development
b. students' gender development
c. students' chronological age
d. students' developmental stage

71. Max fell forward when performing an isometric squat. Which of the following biomechanical factors contributed to this forward motion?

a. the heels are flat
b. the chest is too low
c. the feet are too wide
d. the hips are not far back enough

72. Linda is doing research to help determine how she wants to treat her illness. Which of the following sources should she consider LEAST reliable?

a. An article from a website ending in .edu
b. An article with evidence cited at the bottom of the webpage
c. An article published by the creator of a product used in treatment
d. An article published within the last 18 months

73. Which of the following cardiovascular and endurance training risk-reduction steps can be used in physical education programs?

a. A PAR-Q
b. A talk test
c. A medical waiver
d. A warm-up

74. Which of the following is required equipment for fencing?

a. a singlet
b. a pair of shin guards
c. a foil
d. a large mat

75. During his second year of college, Omarion begins experiencing a growing and overwhelming feeling of hopelessness and notices drastic changes to his sleep patterns. Although he previously had high grades and participated in intramural soccer, he has suddenly lost all interest in going to class or exercising. He lacks motivation to get out of bed and has lost pleasure in most things he used to enjoy doing. After Omarion is evaluated, his doctor diagnoses him with major depressive disorder. Each of the following is a well-documented risk factor for major depressive disorder EXCEPT:

a. History of trauma and/or abuse
b. Perceived social isolation
c. Second-degree relative with a mood disorder
d. Traumatic brain injury

76. Which of the following is an appropriate method used to assess heart rate (HR) intensity during exercise?

a. Continuous aerobic activity
b. Talk test
c. Percentage of maximum heart rate
d. Recovery heart rate

77. The teacher would like to teach the movement concepts effort, relationships, and spatial awareness. Which of the following activities are recommended to develop these concepts?

a. Stationary movements
b. Balancing on the balance beam
c. Fitness activities
d. Animal walks

78. Unhealthy family dynamics are associated with poor attachment, poor communication, and emotional dysregulation. Which of the following risk factors related to family dynamics is LEAST likely to contribute to unhealthy relationships?

a. Rigid expectations of children
b. Intrusive parents
c. Preferential treatment among children
d. Diverse family structures

79. Which of the following statements best describes Bandura's social learning theory?

a. Learning through touch
b. Learning through reading
c. Learning through mental imagery
d. Learning through observation

80. Jimmy wants to improve his cardiovascular fitness by the end of the semester. Which of the following goal setting strategies does Jimmy need to include to monitor his progress toward his final goal?

a. a specific goal
b. a realistic goal
c. a measurable goal
d. an attainable goal

81. Some physical education programs have been cut and threatened with elimination. Which of the following physical activity resources are available to students from diverse communities?

a. Basketball courts
b. Tennis courts
c. After school programs
d. Parks and recreation centers

82. Which of the following is a strategy used to develop locomotor and non-locomotor movements?

a. games
b. equipment
c. choice
d. mirroring

83. In creating a positive climate for PE student learning activities, which of the following accurately reflects an expert recommendation or principle?

a. Increasing learning opportunities creates a positive climate.
b. Teachers must use a few motivational strategies uniformly.
c. Students must already have learned appropriate behaviors.
d. Holding students accountable destroys the positive climate.

84. A student trips over her shoelaces and hits her head on the volleyball standards during gameplay. Which of the following should the teacher have done to reduce the risk of liability?

a. tied the student's shoelaces
b. nothing as it was an accident
c. covered the standards with padding
d. posted the potential risks

85. Which of the following practice styles has been shown to be the most effective in improving student performance in PE and sport settings?

a. Random practice
b. Variable practice
c. Blocked practice
d. Mental practice

86. Which of the following manipulative skills is NOT classified as propulsive?

a. Kicking
b. Striking
c. Catching
d. Throwing

87. Ms. Johnson is in a panic because Mr. Oliver took the heart rate monitors she needs for class. Which of the following heart rate monitoring strategies can the teacher use?

a. taking the pulse rate at the radial artery
b. using the talk test
c. checking rate of perceived exertion
d. asking students how they feel

88. Students have been instructed to set their heart rate monitors in their target heart rate zone (THRZ) using their heart rate reserve (HRR) and intensity range between 65% to 85%. Which of the following illustrates Xiaomi's target heart rate zone as a 16-year-old with a resting heart rate of 82 bpm?

a. 133 bpm to 173 bpm
b. 161 bpm to 186 bpm
c. 204 bpm to 220 bpm
d. 186 bpm to 220 bpm

89. Which safety rule is unique to golf, archery, and racquet activities?

a. Maintaining distance from striker or shooter
b. Avoiding facing the person striking or shooting the object
c. Keeping one's eyes on the object
d. Looking before releasing or striking

90. Which of the following distinguishes etiquette between individual and team sports?

a. personal vs. team fouls
b. no coaching vs. coaching
c. no noise vs. loud noise
d. no penalty cards vs. yellow and red cards

Constructed Response

91. Use the graphic below to complete the exercise that follows.

USDA MyPlate

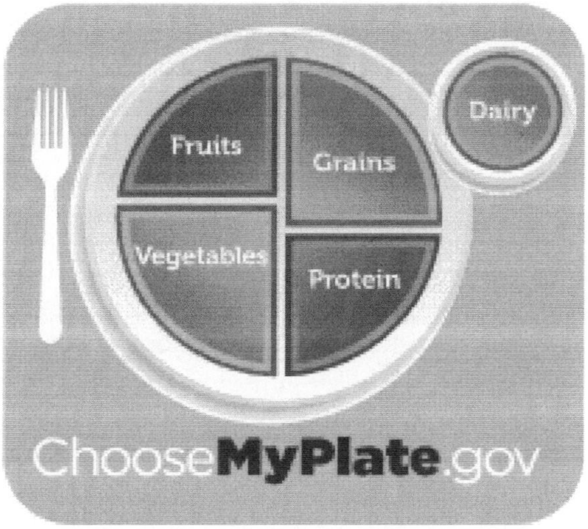

The USDA introduced the MyPlate graphic to provide guidance to Americans regarding healthy eating choices. Using your knowledge of childhood nutrition requirements:

- Create a daily meal plan for an 8-year-old child that aligns with the recommendations included in MyPlate.
- Identify one struggle that a parent or guardian may face while preparing and serving a meal aligned with the nutritional recommendations of MyPlate.
- Explain one solution that will encourage children to make healthy and nutritious food choices.

Answer Key and Explanations for Test #2

Selected Response

1. A: Some students and others may be pleasantly surprised to learn that overweight and obese individuals can lower their risk of related diseases by losing only 5-10 percent of their existing body weight. In addition, overweight (not obese) individuals whose waist measurements are not disproportionately large and who have one or no other risk factors may need only maintain rather than reduce their weight.

2. C: Eliminating requirements to complete some activities within certain time limits reflects a curricular adaptation for special-needs students in the area of rules. Lowering a basketball hoop (a) reflects a modification in the area of equipment. Installing padding and hand holds (b), as well as making other adaptive equipment accessible, are modifications in the area of environment. Giving oral prompts (d) reflects modification in the area of directions.

3. B: The student has not developed emotional self-regulation, which is the ability to control emotions, usually developed by age six. Emotional knowledge is recognizing the emotional state of another. Self-efficacy is the personal belief or confidence in performing a skill. Self-esteem is how one feels about themselves, which can be high/positive or low/negative.

4. A: Katherine should incorporate lateral deltoid raises to target the shoulders and shrugs to target the trapezius (the muscle group connecting the neck and shoulders) to prepare for the swim season. Deltoid raises can be performed laterally, posteriorly, and anteriorly, but lateral deltoid raises also work the trapezius muscles. Shoulder joint actions include flexion, extension, adduction, and abduction, but the shoulder joint is not capable of a curling action.

5. C: Planks work the trunk (abs and back), and squats work the quadriceps. Curl-ups train the abdominals, and deadlifts train the hamstrings. Knee lifts train the abdominals and quadriceps, and seated rows train the back muscles (lats and rhomboids). Twists work the abdominals, and leg curls work the hamstrings. There are synergistic muscle groups involved in most exercises, but the dominant muscle groups worked are identified.

6. C: Abilities predominantly result from the genetic make-up of an individual, which varies among students in physical education. With practice, most individuals can improve their motor skills, but the degree of improvement is contingent upon their abilities.

7. C: Outdoor or alternative spaces such as recreation rooms and stages should be considered to help alleviate overcrowding of teaching spaces, since too many students in one space increases the risk of injury. Team teaching is a strategy that can be used that allows teachers to teach to their strengths but is usually done when two classes share space rather than if multiple classes are in a confined space. Reducing course offerings prevents students from receiving a well-rounded physical education program and threatens to further eliminate physical education programming.

8. B: Metabolic syndrome is a medical condition related to sedentary lifestyles and poor nutritional habits that includes three or more risk factors including obesity, high cholesterol, hypertension (high blood pressure), high glucose (high blood sugar), and excessive fat around the waist. All of these factors occur in a cluster which increases the risk of diabetes, stroke, and heart disease. Hypokinetic diseases are also lifestyle conditions that result from inactivity or sedentary living that include the risk factors of metabolic syndrome as well as osteoarthritis, osteoporosis, some cancers, depression, and lower-back pain.

9. C: Mr. Green can reduce the time it takes for attendance by taking it when students are engaged in an activity like the warm-up or instant activity. Setting an attendance time-limit will not likely decrease the time as 40 students need to be accounted for. Mr. Green could practice but practicing a managerial tool takes away from planning for instruction/learning. Squad lines where students sit or stand in the same spot make it easier to see absent students but unless a warm-up or activity is conducted in the squad lines, students have to wait to be engaged in activities.

10. B: In abusive relationships, when an abuser apologizes and acts normal, he or she is usually not genuinely sorry and does not intend to change. Abusers may blame the victim for causing the abuse, or they may apologize, which is not a sign the victim can believe him or her. In spite of apologies, the abuser is likely to repeat the abuse.

11. C: According to the DECIDE model, the most appropriate first step is to define the problem. Yeslia should consult with the employee to define the challenges that he or she faces and any stressors causing his or her loss of productivity.

12. A: In responding to inevitable conflicts, experts find it healthier to see the reciprocal benefits of directly confronting them than to avoid conflicts for fear of negative outcomes (C). They find people who remain calm, show respect for others, and avoid defensiveness manage conflict more healthily than those who react emotionally by exploding, venting anger (B), expressing resentment, or intentionally hurting others' feelings. Being able and willing to compromise is a healthier response to conflict than refusing to see others' viewpoints (D).

13. B: Students in grades K-2 should be able to demonstrate progress toward more complexity in manipulative motor skills (C). Students in grades 3-5 should be able to refine and apply complex manipulative skills in the context of lead-up games (A). Students in grades 6-8 should be able to apply basic and advanced manipulative skills to sports, dance, and gymnastics, individually and on teams (D). Students in grades 9-12 should be able to create their own advanced movement skills and use them (B).

14. B: While even mild (A) exercise is better than none, and moderate (C) exercise prevents a great variety of illnesses, researchers have found aerobic exercise at a vigorous intensity level the most beneficial specifically to protect the cardiovascular system against coronary heart disease. Therefore, (D) is incorrect.

15. D: Recognizing and understanding the significance of regular physical activity to healthy lifestyles is an objective most appropriate for grades 6-12 in public schools. For grades EC-K (A), recognizing that physical activity has health benefits is more appropriate. For K-2 (B), recognizing the benefits of moderate to vigorous physical activity is appropriate. For grades 3-5 (C), recognizing and applying essential movement concepts and elements for their own sustained participation in physical activities is appropriate.

16. D: The body will turn slowest with the greatest radius of rotation, and fastest with the smallest rotation radius. Extending the arms creates the longest radius; therefore, the body turns *more* slowly, not less, with arms extended (A). In the pike position, the body turns at a medium speed (B); pulling the arms in toward the body shortens the radius, causing faster rotation. So the body turns fastest in full tuck position (C), and slowest in lay-out position (D).

17. C: Body awareness is fundamental to many other skills that students need in school. Children with good awareness of their own body parts, how those parts can move, and their bodies' relationship to their surroundings develop good motor skills, which directly lead to developing good perceptual skills, not vice versa (A). Gross motor skills develop first, leading to fine motor skills development, not vice versa (B). Reading, writing, and other learning are supported by both motor and perceptual skills (D).

18. B: A basketball game requires open motor skills because the environment is unpredictable. In open settings, the individual is not in complete control and makes decisions based on teammates (offenses) and opponents (defenses). In contrast, golf is a closed motor skill where the individual has complete control when deciding to strike the ball. Tennis takes place in an open-skill environment, but the tennis serve is a closed skill as the server controls the movement. Gymnastics is a closed motor skill environment as the gymnast decides when and how to move and is not reliant on others.

19. A: WIC programs are government nutritional subsidies for women, infants, and children. WIC enrollment is typically performed at local health agencies (e.g., WIC office, local health department, social service agencies). A school health clinic practitioner may refer a parent to a WIC enrollment location. School-based health clinics provide a range of health services (e.g., mental health, eye and dental care, sick visits, sports physicals, and health education). However, they should not be used as a replacement for primary care.

20. B: For exercise to be aerobic, it must involve continuous movement, not stop-and-start movement, to elevate the heart and respiratory rates for sustained durations. Aerobic exercise uses the large muscle groups, not small (a). It typically does NOT firm or tone muscles (c) due to low resistance; weight training does. Another common misconception is that aerobic exercise must be of low intensity to burn fat (d); research finds sufficient exercise at any intensity can reduce fat.

21. B: Spectators are engaging in poor etiquette as it is an expectation that fans and spectators are quiet during stokes. Booing at any moment during a golf tournament is also considered poor etiquette. Taunting is intentional behavior designed to insult or provoke someone. The spectators are not breaking any rules, but the practice of booing is strongly discouraged and considered poor taste. While the golfer is a woman, there is not enough information to determine if the booing is related to sex or gender.

22. A: Modeling expected behaviors is a strategy that reduces student conflict. Students often engage in behaviors they see rather than the ones they told are correct. Peer mediation is a strategy used to solve student conflict after it has already occurred. Separating students might be a temporary measure used as a cooling-off period but is also implemented after the conflict. Furthermore, cooperation and working with others are fundamental objectives in most physical education programs, and separating students is not an appropriate long-term solution. Calling the parents is an informative response to conflict that has already transpired but is unnecessary to conduct before any potential conflict.

23. C: The rationale behind incorporating movement concepts is to make movements more visually appealing or aesthetic, which aids in developing mature movement patterns used in dance. All lessons should aim to accommodate multiple abilities and to keep students interested. Dance is conducted for various reasons such as artistic passion, social activity, cultural expression, and health maintenance, but the purpose of adding movement concepts is to foster mature movement patterns.

24. D: Generally, students learn PE skills better by viewing and imitating demonstrations (A) than hearing explanations or descriptions, but demonstration by itself works best for students with mainly visual learning styles. Students with logical, mathematical, or visual learning styles benefit from adding diagrams to demonstrations (B). Students with kinesthetic learning styles benefit from being physically guided through skill movements in addition to seeing them demonstrated (C). Students with verbal learning styles benefit from adding spoken explanations or descriptions to demonstrations (D).

25. A: Large-scale state research has found that student cardiovascular fitness achievement and healthy body mass index (BMI) scores correlate positively with student scores on the state academic achievement test of knowledge and skills. Other research has found that children who are more physically fit demonstrate not only quicker reaction times but also more accurate responses (B). Another investigation found that children burn more calories and take nearly twice as many steps during teacher-led fitness activities as during active gaming, not vice versa (C). Other studies show that intense exercise is followed by improvement in cognitive function (D).

26. C: Aside from medication compliance and individual therapy, the most effective treatment strategy is supportive family therapy. Supportive family therapy instructs families on how to best support their loved one with schizophrenia, identify signs and symptoms that indicate an impending relapse, educate family members on medication and treatment, and provide emotional support to family members. It promotes empathy and strong social ties within the family unit, which will help reduce hospital readmission and symptom relapse and improve the overall social-emotional functioning of the patient.

27. C: The short-term effects of regular, substantial alcohol use include impaired judgment (A); distortion of perceptions, vision and hearing (B), and emotions; impaired coordination; bad breath; and hangovers. The long-term effects of heavy alcohol use include liver damage, sexual impotence, stomach disorders (D), vitamin deficiencies, skin problems, loss of appetite, loss of memory, damage to the heart and entire cardiovascular system, and damage to the central nervous system (C).

28. B: Dribbling a basketball around stationary objects, using both hands, demonstrates mature form in manipulative skills. Combining locomotor and non-locomotor skills, changing pace, level, and direction in a 1-minute dance (A) demonstrate basic competence in more complex movement skills for sport-specific activities. Throwing different distances through different forces and trajectories (C) demonstrates identifying basic concepts applying to skills the student is practicing. Keeping a log of practice throws, contrasting first to last attempts (D), demonstrates explaining how performance improves through practicing movement skills.

29. C: In the first cognitive stage of motor learning, learners understand the activity's goal and nature (A) and make initial attempts to perform it that include major errors (B). In the second associative stage, learners engage in practice to master the timing of the skill, and they make fewer errors that are more consistent in nature (C). In the third autonomous stage, learners perform the activity effortlessly and automatically (D), enabling them to redirect their attention to other aspects of the skill.

30. B: School emergency procedures typically provide that injured students are initially offered first aid by physical educators with current first aid certification, and only seen by a school nurse for follow-up as needed (A); that all physical educators carry emergency first aid kits during PE classes (B); that ALL physical educators must have current first aid and CPR certification (C); and that PE teachers and other physical educators have a list of any students who did not return emergency treatment permission forms the first week of school (D).

31. C: Students may go under, over, toward, away from, in front of, behind, and beside (A) and (B), but not inside or outside of these. Students can go into, out of, toward, away from, next to, or in front of (D), but not over, under, and often not behind such rooms. However, with differently sized boxes or hoops (C), they can explore all of these relationships, including going inside and outside of them.

32. A: The Presidential Youth Fitness and FitnessGram® programs are designed to assess health-related fitness, including muscular endurance, muscular strength, cardiovascular endurance, flexibility, and body composition, as these components impact life quality. Skill-related fitness (B) is sport-related or performance skills and includes power, agility, coordination, speed, reaction time, and balance. Fitness assessments that measure both skills- and health-related fitness (C) are assessments used for military entry and training, including the candidate fitness test. Dynamic and non-dynamic or static activities (D) are conducted in the Presidential Youth and FitnessGram® assessments but do not include sports skills.

33. C: The overhand throw is a manipulative movement skill that combines non-locomotor or locomotor movement with an object or equipment. Locomotor movements are traveling movements that get a person from point A to point B. Non-locomotor movements are movements without traveling. While weight transfer is done during the overhand throw, weight transfer is a movement concept and not a fundamental skill category.

34. C: The Red Cross's mission is to help vulnerable communities prepare for, respond to, and recover from life- or health-threatening conditions. The National Guard is responsible for assisting with evacuation during natural disasters. The Food and Drug Administration (FDA) oversees the manufacturing of supplements. Doctors Without Borders is the most well-known organization that provides healthcare abroad.

35. D: According to research findings, adolescents must have practice with making decisions in real life to transfer the cognitive skills they have acquired for decision making to reality. Studies identify that variables influencing teen decision-making skills include their levels of conformity with parental or peer norms (A); demographic characteristics like age, race, ethnicity, gender, social class; and family dynamics, family structure, and personal characteristics like intelligence and temperament as well (B). Research also shows that adolescents tend to be more oriented to the present and short-term consequences and goals and need to be taught future orientation, long-term goals (C), and planning.

36. C: Individual risk factors for IPV include low education, low socioeconomic status, drug use, impulsivity, poor behavior management skills, history of experiencing abuse, hostility toward the opposite gender, stress, and social isolation. Relationship risk factors include witnessing abuse between parents, disrupted family dynamics (e.g., divorce, separation), and friendships with aggressive or violent peers. Community risk factors include high poverty rates, limited economic opportunities, high unemployment, high crime rates, and high rates of drug use. High self-esteem is generally a protective factor.

37. B: An increase in ventilation or breathing is an acute or immediate response to aerobic exercise. A lower resting heart rate is a long-term physiological response to aerobic exercise. Cardiac output remains constant during long sessions of aerobic exercise. Cardiac output and stroke volume (the amount of blood ejected from the left and right ventricle due to the contraction of the heart) increases are also acute responses to aerobic exercise.

38. A: One common unhealthy reaction to stress is pain, such as headaches, backaches, stomach aches, muscular aches from unconsciously tensing or clenching muscles, and other physical symptoms. People are far more likely to begin or resume using substances than quit using them in reaction to stress. Changes in eating are also common reactions to stress: Some individuals overeat and gain weight, while others skip eating and lose weight (B). Anger and crying are also equally common reactions (C). Symptoms of anxiety, depression, or both are also common unhealthy reactions to stress (D).

39. A: Young people generally feel themselves to be invincible and show little regard for the future consequences of their behavior. More immediate concerns are shortages of cash, romantic rejection, and athletic inadequacy.

40. C: According to PE experts, self-assessment has great power as a tool in student motor skills development, because requiring students to assess their own abilities and skills encourages them to reflect, which does NOT interfere with executing the skills (b), but does enable them to determine their current skill levels (c), as well as to take, not lose, control of the developmental process (d). Students need not be PE teachers or have specialized training to conduct self-assessment (a).

41. A: Preparing equipment ahead of time increases instructional time. Observing students who look fatigued is a safety measure to ensure students have adequate rest and water breaks. Wearing a watch and adhering to the bell schedule can help track the time of activities, but they do not increase instructional time.

42. C: Implementing family-friendly work policies (e.g., remote work, paid childcare, flexible work schedule) is an example of strengthening economic supports to families because these policies allow parents to fulfill their duties as an employee and caregiver more effectively. Higher minimum wages are also an example of strengthening economic supports.

43. A: To attain the fastest acceleration, a sprinter should keep the center of gravity as high as possible while crouching in the starting block. As the sprinter accelerates, the upper body rises with forward body propulsion. Having the center of gravity lowest (b), between high and low (c), or starting in the full upright body position (d) will allow less speed in accelerating.

44. D: Exploring the basics of these skills (a) most applies to students in grades K-2. Demonstrating mature forms of these skills (b) most applies to students in grades 3-5. Applying those mature forms in more specialized PE areas (c) most applies to students in grades 6-8. Using these motor skills for activities in these areas (d) most applies to students in grades 9-12.

45. C: Reaction time is a perceptual motor ability as it uses the senses and is dependent on the environment, such as a starting gun in track or having to play defense. Muscular strength is reliant on physiological factors and is less dependent on the environment, such as a student's coordination or ability to do push-ups.

46. B: Resistance skills against peer pressure to engage in risky behaviors exemplify social and psychological life skills that PE promotes, according to the President's Council on Physical Fitness and Sports, which also identifies improved developmental outcomes from PE including motivation, self-confidence (A), self-regulation (C), and perseverance (D).

47. A: Researchers have found that smaller class sizes and student–teacher ratios correlate with larger quantities of activity time, activity level, safety, and learning for students, whereas larger class sizes and student–teacher ratios correlate with smaller quantities of student activity times, levels, safety, and learning—that is, an inverse correlation. Studies show that students receive more and better physical education (PE) from teachers who teach only PE rather than dividing their teaching time and attention between PE and other subjects (B). Researchers are coming to increasing consensus that standards-based PE curriculum results in greater student physical activity (C). Well-maintained, safe, appropriate, and aesthetically appealing PE facilities and equipment also are found to increase and improve student activity (D).

48. B: Force or effort is the most emphasized movement concept in the leap as it requires power on the take-off, and force is absorbed on the landing while maintaining body control. Rhythm is the movement concept that helps students develop creative movements to music or sounds, e.g., a drum beat. Time is the movement rate and is used across locomotor movements but is not the leap's dominant movement concept. The leap is performed at a medium or high level.

49. B: Integrated physical education is a cross-curricular approach where two or more areas of study are taught together. In this example, students may not only learn how to perform the overhand throw (biomechanics), but may also learn about the angle of release, projectile motion, and force (Physics). Exercise and sport science are sub-disciplines of kinesiology that study human movement in exercise and sport settings. Physical education is also a sub-discipline of kinesiology that studies human movement in schools or pedagogy.

50. C: A physiological benefit of exercise is it lowers the release of cortisol–a stress hormone and increases the release of endorphins–happy hormones. These physiological responses promote psychological outcomes or benefits including improved mood, positive thoughts, and increased confidence. Confidence also results from seeing the physical changes the body goes through from engaging in exercise.

51. D: Answers A, B, and C are all positive coping skills that can ease the stress related to the student's test. Putting limits on activities and refraining from well-needed breaks can add to the stress the student is already experiencing.

52. D: Jason has difficulty with kinesthetic discrimination, which requires identifying small movements in large gross motor activities. These are small movements of gross motor muscle groups and not fine motor movements with the hands and feet. Auditory discrimination is the ability to distinguish between sounds that are important and unimportant. Visual discrimination is the ability to distinguish objects, colors, shapes, and sizes.

53. D: Trunk lifts will help Daniel strengthen his core, including the lower back. Lat pulls train the latissimus dorsi, which is the large part of the upper back. One-arm rows also train the latissimus dorsi and the rhomboids or the upper inner parts of the back. The seated row also targets the latissimus dorsi and rhomboids.

54. A: James lacks flexibility in the ankles or the ability to lift his toes towards his shin (dorsiflexion). Toe raises, also known as heel or calf raises, and drops will help James increase his ankle flexibility. The lack of hip flexibility may also cause lifting of the heels, but deadlifts target the hamstrings and lower back. Static and dynamic or a combination of active and passive hip stretching exercises, such as butterflies, kneeling lunges, and pigeons, will help with hip flexibility. Plantar extension is pointing the toes downward, which is not an issue for James as his toes must contact the floor for the heels to lift. Poor knee strength is the weakness in the muscles surrounding the knee, which would prevent James from performing the squat correctly. Side, lateral, and reverse lunges, step-ups, and wall-sits at 90 degrees help strengthen the knee's muscles.

55. A: Assertive communication is the most effective communication style. Those who practice assertive communication can communicate their needs and feelings in a considerate manner while also respecting the needs of others. Aggressive communicators are often loud and demanding. They may use intimidation tactics to attain control over others. Passive communicators suppress their feelings and needs to avoid confrontation. Passive-aggressive communicators may outwardly display passive nonverbal or verbal communication techniques yet indirectly express negative or aggressive feelings.

56. A: Ari can help keep the ball inbounds by adding topspin, which will cause the ball to drop downward instead of going out of bounds. This is achieved by moving the striking arm from low to high with follow-through over the opposite shoulder. Increasing the speed of the racket may result in the ball traveling farther out. Stroke technique and contact point are more impactful than the amount of power placed on the ball.

57. B: Setting team goals fosters teamwork since, ideally, all members agree and are committed to working towards the same goal. Team captains help lead and can remind players of the common goals, but this is not the best strategy to foster teamwork, as not all teams have captains. Meeting with players individually is more appropriate for individual goal setting or to inform players of behaviors counter to teamwork, such as not passing the ball. Watching videos can help identify and provide feedback regarding teamwork, but setting goals and expectations must occur for this to be an effective strategy.

58. D: While Tufts University is a reliable source for health information, the .biz domain indicates that it may not be a reliable site. University sites in the US generally use the .edu domain. Other domain endings do not necessarily indicate the information listed is false, but they should be validated using an additional trusted source. The .biz domain could be an indication that the site is an impersonation or commercial site.

59. A: The self-determination theory is a psychological approach used to teach physical education to increase intrinsic student motivation by providing students with achievable but challenging tasks. Intrinsic motivation has shown most effective in fostering appreciation and lifelong physical activity engagement. Behaviorism focuses on the psychomotor domain and is a teacher-directed approach that works to change students' behaviors based on the environment the teacher creates. Social theory relies heavily on the affective domain, or the social aspects of student engagement, and underpins cooperative and sport education models where students work together to solve problems. Constructivism theory focuses on the cognitive domain and works toward providing students with an understanding of what they are doing and why in the psychomotor and affective domains.

60. B: Video analysis has been shown to be the most effective form of feedback for skill performance, as the performer can visually see how they perform a skill. Video analysis is further enhanced when combined with verbal feedback. Performers benefit further when their performance can be viewed alongside the desired movement/skill.

61. D: An effective strategy is having the player sit out the next game to serve as a consequence for missing the workouts. Running laps or performing push-ups is an inappropriate discipline practice as it associates physical activity with pain and punishment. Setting goals is an effective strategy that can be used to accomplish fitness outcomes but is not a disciplinary measure.

62. A: The numerous benefits of physical activity engagement are why physical activity is promoted in physical education programs. Consistent physical activity engagement reduces the risk of heart disease and other health conditions and improves mental health outcomes. Physical activity reduces blood pressure. Sedentary activities and poor dietary intake increase blood pressure risks. Engaging in muscular fitness activities lead to muscle hypertrophy and prevents atrophy or the wasting of muscle. Endorphins or "happy hormones" are released during physical activity which is another benefit of physical activity.

63. D: To improve muscular endurance, one should engage in lifting low weight at high repetitions (reps) as the goal is to prepare the muscles to work for long periods of time e.g., running marathons and holding planks and squats. To improve muscular strength, one should engage in high weight and low reps to allow for muscle hypertrophy. When training for muscular endurance, muscular strength improves but at a slower rate. When training for muscular strength, muscular endurance also improves but more slowly, as the training is specific to the muscular strength goal.

64. D: Verbal communication is the primary means of communication, whereas nonverbal communication is frequently used to reinforce messages or convey unspoken information (e.g., raising eyebrows to show surprise, maintaining eye contact to show active listening). Nonverbal communication consists of body language and facial expressions, and it can be intentional or unintentional.

65. D: Students are likely to improve if they "see" themselves perform the cartwheel with bent legs to help them focus when they perform the cartwheel, again. Observations and skill cues are usually the first stages of instruction, so it is evident that these options have not helped. Since students are already flexible, yoga would not be an activity that would help them improve.

66. B: Zigzag running or alternating diagonal patterns are common in dual and team sports. Transitions occur in dual and team sports, but it is the transition from offense to defense and vice versa with footwork patterns differing across sport types. Curve patterns are not common in dual and team sports. Some team sports have high-level movements like jumping in volleyball and basketball, but dual sports such as tennis and badminton, use mostly medium-level movements but not defensive running patterns.

67. A: Personal space is the focus of dancing freely in a contained area. General space is dancing freely around the gym or in an open space that belongs to no one or everyone. Varying spaces are different areas or types of space. For example, the teacher instructs half of the class to move in open space and restricts the other half to personal space movements. There can be an area for personal space activities and an area with general space activities or alternating between personal space (pause and bend) and general space (run). There are non-locomotor activities in personal space, but non-locomotor space is a fundamental movement skill and not a spatial awareness movement concept.

68. D: It is during Stage 4 that talent, among other factors, plays a role in how a person continues to develop motor skills. Other relevant factors include how highly a person is motivated and how often a person practices the motor skills in question. Stage 4 is the last stage of motor development, during which one hones existing skills, as well as learns more complicated skills (for example, refining a golf swing to hit the ball in just the right way). In prior stages of motor development, talent does not play a particular role in how a person develops motor skills.

69. B: Adequate opportunities to respond (OTR) or practicing skills regularly aid in skill refinement. Tag games keep students physically active and help teach movement concepts including speed, dodging, fleeing, and chasing. Leading and following are strategies that aid in the refinement of locomotor skills. Choice is a strategy used to foster motivation to participate.

70. D: Students' stages of development must be considered for effective planning. Chronological age is important and there are certain markers of motor and cognitive skill ability, but students of the same age are at diverse learning stages. While there are sex differences, stages of development include variations across groups, as there can be boys and girls with mixed or the same abilities at the same age within and across group categories. Gender development differs from sex as these are social and cultural expectations placed on individuals according to sex at birth, such as blue for boys and pink for girls, which may conflict with one's gender identity, e.g., transgender, or non-binary.

71. D: Max's hips are not far back enough during his squat, causing him to lose balance or stability. The heels should be flat as squatting on the toes can also create a forward motion. At one time, deep squats below 90 degrees were frowned upon, but new research indicates that a deep squat performed correctly is safe and does not impact balance. Max is likely to fall back if the chest is too low, which puts more weight in the rear, thus pulling him backward. A lifted chest with the hips back counters this effect.

72. C: An article published by the creator of a product used in treatment would most likely be biased. More reliable information that has been peer reviewed should be used for research. A website ending in .edu is associated with a university. This will likely have been reviewed by health professionals associated with the university. Evidence used in an article should be cited at the bottom so consumers can access original sources. An article published within the last 18 months is considered current. Information used to make healthcare decisions should be current to ensure it is in accordance with related best practices.

73. A: Although student health risks are generally shared with physical education teachers from school personnel, administering a Physical Activity Readiness Questionnaire (PAR-Q) is a simple proactive measure to identify potential health risks associated with cardiovascular and endurance training. A PAR-Q asks students/participants/parents to respond to health history questions that may negatively impact activity such as a history of asthma or musculoskeletal injuries. Athletics and sports programs require physicals for participation, but they are generally not required in physical education programs. A proper warm-up reduces the risk of injury as it prepares the body for vigorous activity when engaging in cardiovascular activities. However, a warm-up does not identify potential health risks. A talk test is a self-evaluation of exercise intensity.

74. C: The sword in fencing is called a foil. Soccer, cricket, lacrosse, hockey, and baseball use shin guards. Wrestlers wear a singlet, and players compete on a large mat. Tumbling and gymnastics also occur on large mats.

75. C: Risk factors for major depressive disorder include adverse childhood experiences (e.g., death of a loved one, abuse, trauma), low social support, and traumatic brain injuries. A person with a first-degree relative (e.g., parent, sibling) has a two to three times greater risk of developing major depressive disorder. There is little evidence demonstrating an association between second-degree relatives (e.g., aunt, uncle, grandparents) and an increased risk of developing a mood disorder like major depressive disorder.

76. C: Training at a percentage of the maximum heart rate (MHR) is used to assess heart rate intensity during exercise. For cardiovascular fitness, working at 65 to 85% of the MHR is the recommended range, with beginners starting at the lower limits and advanced exercisers working at the upper limits. Elite endurance athletes or those with high cardiovascular fitness can work at 90% of MHR. Continuous aerobic activity is a method to determine the time and/or distance of the activity. The talk test aids in determining relative intensity based on if one can or cannot talk or sing during cardiovascular activities. If one is unable to talk, the intensity is too high for continuous activity. If one can talk but not sing, the intensity is at a moderate level. If they can sing, the intensity is too low. Recovery heart rate is the time it takes for the heart to return to normal or rest after activity and is one way to measure cardiovascular improvements. The fitter one becomes, the faster the heart rate returns to normal.

77. D: Animal walks are recommended to teach these movement concepts as students can draw on prior knowledge of how animals move. Using animals allows students to identify different concepts, such as "moving like a flock of birds," to understand spatial awareness, effort, and relationships. Although stationary movements and balancing can teach some movement concepts, the lack of variety limits what can be taught. Fitness activities can teach some movement concepts, but fitness concepts are more abstract and will likely confuse younger children.

78. D: Diverse family structures refer to different formations of family beyond the conventional nuclear family. Examples include single-parent, foster-parent, or adoptive parent families; blended families (e.g., half siblings, relatives by marriage); non-parent relatives or intergenerational households; or LGBT parents. Although some family structures may increase stress (e.g., single-parent households) due to the loss of a caregiver or financial security, diverse family structures are not associated with producing unhealthy relationships.

79. D: Bandura's social learning theory is also known as observational learning theory, where watching someone's performance through modeling and demonstration as well as receiving feedback impact learning. Learning through touch, reading, and mental imagery also aid in learning but are not a part of observational learning theory.

80. C: Jimmy needs to include a trackable measure for his cardiovascular fitness goal to determine if the goal has been met. For example, a measurable goal is "I want to improve my cardiovascular fitness by being able to jog for 20-minutes without stopping." With consistent progressive overload such as gradually increasing the jogging time until reaching 20-minutes or working on cardiovascular fitness, the goal is realistic and attainable as it is a semester-long goal.

81. D: Parks and recreation centers are resources available to students from diverse communities that are either free, inexpensive, or have sliding scale fees based on socio-economics. Some schools have after-school programs, but not all offer physical activity programs. After school programs also cost extra resources and require that parents provide alternative transportation methods, and not all students live in the communities where they attend school. Basketball and tennis courts are available in some neighborhoods and are generally not supervised unless a part of the parks and recreation centers.

82. D: Mirroring is when partners face each other. One partner does what the other is doing, which aids in the development of locomotor and non-locomotor movements as students have an opportunity to "see" and imitate or "mirror" the movement. Mirroring is helpful to unskilled students who can mirror skilled students. Skilled students also benefit from mirroring drills as they can detect and correct errors, which helps both the skilled and unskilled students become proficient. Choice is a strategy used to foster motivation. There are multiple purposes for games, but games allow students to put skills into practice. Equipment aids in the development of movement concepts and manipulative skills.

83. A: Experts at PE Central say one way PE teachers can create a positive climate for student activity and learning is to increase the opportunities for students to learn. They also say creating this positive climate requires using many varied motivational strategies (b), helping students learn and sustain appropriate behaviors (c), and promoting student responsibility and accountability (d).

84. C: The teacher should make sure that the standards were covered with padding to reduce the risk of liability as it is a foreseeable risk. It is not the teacher's responsibility to tie a student's shoes, but if the teacher notices that a student's shoelaces are untied, she should inform the student to tie them or tie them if the student does not know how. The student tripping over the shoelaces was an accident, but if the standards are uncovered, the teacher may be held liable for an injury. Safety rules rather than potential risks should be posted.

85. B: Variable practice has been shown to be the most effective in PE and sport settings, as the same game skills are practiced in various situations to mimic real play, e.g., small-sided games. Random practice is mixing up skills in random order, which is similar to variable practice, but the skills differ. Blocked practice focuses on one skill at a time and repeats, which is evident during isolation skills practice. Mental practice is thinking about or rehearsing the skill cognitively, which has been shown to benefit physical skills when used in conjunction with physical practice, but it is not as strong when used independently.

86. C: Catching is a manipulative skill that is classified as receptive, i.e., the catcher *receives* a moving ball or other object that another player has thrown, kicked, or stricken. Kicking (a), striking (b), and throwing (d) are all manipulative skills classified as propulsive, i.e., a player *propels* the ball or other object to make it move through the air, across a surface, etc.

87. A: Ms. Johnson can have students take their pulse at the radial or carotid arteries to measure heart rate. The talk test helps determine if the activities are too easy or intense, but it does not measure heart rate. The rate of perceived exertion is another tool used to determine or evaluate the intensity of exercises but is not a heart rate measurement. Asking students how they feel is a great tool to check in to assess students' responses to activities but is not a tool to measure heart rate.

88. B: Xiaomi's target heart rate zone using heart rate reserve (HRR) or the Karvonen method is 161 bpm to 186 bpm. 220-age = maximum heart rate (MHR) (220-16 = 204 bpm). Xiaomi's maximum heart rate is 204 bpm. To compute HRR, subtract resting heart rate from maximum heart rate, which is 204-82 = 122 bpm. Xiaomi's HRR is 122 bpm. The HRR is then multiplied by the target percentages to yield the THRZ of 161 bpm to 186 bpm. The steps to compute Xiaomi's THRZ are:

Step 1: 220 - 16 = 204 bpm	220 - 16 = 204 bpm
Step 2: 204 – 82 bpm = 122 bpm	204 – 82 bpm = 122 bpm
Step 3: 122 x 65% = 79.3	122 x 85% = 103.7
Step 4: 79.3 + 82 = 161.3 bpm	103.7 + 82 = 185.7 bpm

THRZ = 161 bpm – 186 bpm

Xiaomi's THRZ without including HRR would be 133 bpm – 173 bpm.

89. A: Students should be taught to maintain distance from the striker or shooter to avoid getting hit with the striking object such as a golf club, arrow, or ball. While students should avoid facing a person shooting in archery, in racquet sports like tennis and badminton, students face their opponents on opposite sides of the net. Keeping eyes on the ball or the target is an important skill cue; however, it is not a safety rule when striking or shooting. There is no time to look around before striking in racquet activities, in contrast to golf and archery, where the golfer or shooter controls these actions.

90. C: In dual and individual sports, the expectation is that noise is minimal during gameplay. In contrast, during team sports, especially invasion games, loud noise is expected and promoted as fans cheer on their teams. In individual sports, there are only personal fouls and in team sports there are personal and team fouls, but these are rule differences rather than etiquette issues. In tennis, coaches cannot coach players during match play, but coaches can coach the entire game during team sports. These are also rules and not matters of etiquette.

Constructed Response

91. This is the rubric used to score constructed-response questions on the CSET.

Purpose	The extent to which the response addresses the constructed-response assignment's charge in relation to relevant CSET content specifications or subject matter requirements.
Subject Matter Knowledge	Application of accurate subject matter knowledge as described in the relevant CSET content specifications or subject matter requirements.
Support	The appropriateness and quality of the supporting evidence in relation to relevant CSET content specifications or subject matter requirements.

Score Point	Score Point Description
3	**The "3" response reflects command of the relevant knowledge and skills as defined in the CSET content specifications or subject matter requirements.** • The purpose of the assignment is fully achieved. • There is an accurate application of relevant content specifications or subject matter requirements. • There is appropriate and specific relevant supporting evidence.
2	**The "2" response reflects general command of the relevant knowledge and skills as defined in the CSET content specifications or subject matter requirements.** • The purpose of the assignment is largely achieved. • There is a largely accurate application of relevant content specifications or subject matter requirements. • There is acceptable relevant supporting evidence.
1	**The "1" response reflects limited or no command of the relevant knowledge and skills as defined in the CSET content specifications or subject matter requirements.** • The purpose of the assignment is only partially or not achieved. • There is limited or no application of relevant content specifications or subject matter requirements. • There is little or no relevant supporting evidence.
U	**The "U" (unscorable) is assigned to a response that is unrelated to the assignment, illegible, primarily in a language other than English, or does not contain a sufficient amount of original work to score.**
B	**The "B" (blank) is assigned to a response that is blank.**